PATH OF MIRACLES

PATH OF MIRACLES

The Seven Life-Changing Principles That Lead

to Purpose and Fulfillment

SAMUEL RODRIGUEZ

Written with

CARLOS HARRISON

Foreword by Jim Wallis

A CELEBRA BOOK

CELEBRA

Published by New American Library,
a division of Penguin Group (USA) Inc.,
375 Hudson Street, New York, New York 10014, USA
Penguin Group (Canada), 90 Eglinton Avenue East, Suite 700, Toronto,
Ontario M4P 2Y3, Canada (a division of Pearson Penguin Canada Inc.)
Penguin Books Ltd., 80 Strand, London WC2R 0RL, England
Penguin Ireland, 25 St. Stephen's Green, Dublin 2,
Ireland (a division of Penguin Books Ltd.)
Penguin Group (Australia), 250 Camberwell Road, Camberwell,
Victoria 3124, Australia (a division of Pearson Australia Group Pty. Ltd.)
Penguin Books India Pvt. Ltd., 11 Community Centre,
Panchsheel Park, New Delhi – 110 017, India
Penguin Group (NZ), 67 Apollo Drive, Rosedale, North Shore 0632,
New Zealand (a division of Pearson New Zealand Ltd.)
Penguin Books (South Africa) (Pty.) Ltd., 24 Sturdee Avenue,
Rosebank, Johannesburg 2196, South Africa

Penguin Books Ltd., Registered Offices:
80 Strand, London WC2R 0RL, England

First published by Celebra,
a division of Penguin Group (USA) Inc.

First Printing, April 2009
1   3   5   7   9   10   8   6   4   2

CELEBRA and logo are trademarks of Penguin Group (USA) Inc.

LIBRARY OF CONGRESS CATALOGING-IN-PUBLICATION DATA:

Rodriguez, Samuel.
Path of miracles: the seven life-changing principles that lead to purpose and
fulfillment/Samuel Rodriguez with Carlos Harrison.
p.   cm.
ISBN 978-0-451-22644-0
1. Success—Religious aspects—Christianity.   I. Harrison, Carlos.   II. Title.
BV4598.3.R65 2009
248.4—dc22   2008047002

Set in Bulmer MT
Designed by Elke Sigal

Printed in the United States of America

This Book is dedicated to

…the greatest running partner God could have ever blessed me with, my wife Eva. You personify perseverance, integrity, courage and love. Thank you for being the ideal wife, mother, partner, and friend. I can't imagine life without you.

…my greatest miracles, Yvonne, Nathan and Lauren. Your smiles and joy constantly strengthen me. I live to leave something greater for you and your generation. You're not only my children; you are the executive members of the Rodriguez Dream steering committee. Don't forget, if you ever fall, Daddy's there to pick you up.

…My parents, Samuel and Elizabeth. The best possible parents anyone can ever ask for. My father's hands instilled in me a strong work ethic while my mother's wisdom guided me from day one. One of the highlights of my life was the day I found my dad kneeling down praying to the Almighty. This strong, UAW, Mack Truck, powerful man demonstrated that strength comes from above. Mom, seven times around Jericho and the walls will always come down.

…My two sisters, Reina and Lydia. Your covering, love and faithfulness make me thank God daily that I am the youngest and I can always depend upon a firewall of two powerful women of God, my covering. Charlie's Angels? Can I stop playing Bosley now?

…Felix Posos. My tourniquet. I will celebrate with you one day in Heaven. I miss you, Pastor. David Espinoza, my Pastor, thanks for your prayers, support and covering; the Godfather. Dr. Jesse Miranda, we are your children and the heirs of the dream. Thanks for your exemplary leadership. Gilbert Velez, thanks for believing, WOW! Look what God has done. You are a true friend. Nunez, an authentic spiritual father.

The National Hispanic Christian Learning Conference and 3DBN, America's largest Hispanic Christian Organization and a Powerful Global Network of Faith leaders, I am honored to serve you.

...Nick Garza, my Third Day Brother. The Prophetic always trumps the pathetic. Thanks, my Brother!

...The TEAM. Ed and Damaris, Bobby and Liz, Jose and Diana, Ferdinand, Efrain, Oscar, Joshua Perez, Marcos and Monica, Pastor Dan Delgado, Israel "Pastor Jerry," Charlie Rivera, John Raymer, Sam Schneider, David Sandoval, Charlie Olmeda, Daniel Gonzalez, Raul Feliciano, Randy Thomas, Steve Perea, CCA Sacramento and The Assemblies of God Family in America and around the world.

ACKNOWLEDGMENTS

I want to thank Raymond Garcia and the Penguin family for believing in this book and in a Newark, New Jersey, boy raised in Bethlehem, PA, who grew up with a dream. Your professionalism and commitment to excellence stand second to none. In addition, I want to thank Carlos Harrison. You prove that running partners can accomplish greater works together. Please forward the invoice for the sessions; therapy was successful.

Finally, I want to thank the National Hispanic Christian Leadership Conference and 3DBN, along with the Third Day Worship Center Fellowship and my Assemblies of God family, thank you for permitting me to serve and provide a voice for the Hispanic American Faith Community. I stand committed to reconciling both elements of the Cross, the Vertical and Horizontal, both Righteousness and Justice, Kingdom and Society, Covenant and Community, Faith and Public Policy, Billy Graham and Martin Luther King, John 3:16 and Luke 4.

Contents

PRINCIPLE ONE

Life's Greatest Opportunities Arise in Our Darkest Hour

PRINCIPLE TWO

Faith and Fear Always Run Together

Principle Three

God Programmed Us to Have Partners

Principle Four

There's Always an Empty Tomb Right Before a Filled Upper Room

PRINCIPLE FIVE

Order Precedes Promotion

PRINCIPLE SIX

There Is Transformation, Followed by Recognition

PRINCIPLE SEVEN

You Are Assured a Filled Upper Room

FOREWORD

Sam Rodriguez is a unique Christian leader. Not just anybody gets described as "what happens when you put Billy Graham and Martin Luther King Jr. in a blender and put salsa on top."

The face and faith of Evangelicals in this country continues to change. Over 37 percent of our country's Hispanic population identifies as an evangelical. It's what Sam calls the "browning" of the Evangelical movement. If current trends hold true, the majority of evangelical Christians in this country will be of Hispanic descent by the middle of this century. If you want to know about these changes, take a look at Sam. He is the only Christian leader I know who has not only led immigration reform rallies but has also been the commencement speaker for Liberty University. Christianity in our country will never be the same.

What supports this change and is the underlying premise of the book is that the Christian faith is both vertical and horizontal. God's call for the Church and mission for our lives is to live in the place where personal piety and communal piety intersect. It is in this place that we see God's miracles.

Too often, when we hear the word "miracle," we think of a god who does magic tricks to get us the things that we want. If only we are good enough and follow all the right rules, God just might give us everything on our wish list. Sam through his work and his book shows us that most miracles are the everyday realities that occur when we allow the Kingdom of God to touch down to Earth through us.

Our ability to work side by side building the Kingdom, even when we disagree, shows the strength of diversity and the beauty of harmonization without homogenization. It is through learning from others that are different than ourselves that we are able to truly see ourselves.

My most recent book, *The Great Awakening*, is known by a different title in its international releases, *Seven Ways to Change the World*. Sam's seven life-changing principles, if followed, will change the world. The principles are simple and painted with a prose that is accessible to all but may the reader beware. The principles that change the world may be simple, but they are never easy. *Path of Miracles* is a guide to faith from one of the most hopeful young Christian leaders of our time.

—JIM WALLIS

PATH OF MIRACLES

Chapter 1

THE PATH OF MIRACLES

Prepare yourself: Your life is about to change.

You are about to discover the way to a life full of accomplishment, achievement, and attainment, of realization, reward, and prosperity. Of healthy and happy relationships, and lasting love. Of satisfying work and success on the job. Of building wealth and financial freedom.

Right now.

This book will show you how. I will be your guide.

Rick Warren talks about purpose and Joel Osteen talks about the end picture. I'm the guy in the middle. I'm the guy describing the road. I'm the one here to teach you the process.

God has a marathon of miracles waiting for you to enjoy right now, in this lifetime, and the seven simple principles in this book will show you how to unlock the power within you and secure those treasures right here, right now.

You'll see your dreams come true, in ways beyond your wildest imagination—not just fulfilled, but *surpassed*. This is the recipe. This is the how-to. I will show you the way. I will teach you how to have a life that is exceedingly, abundantly, above all you ever wished for. You will discover the "Wow! Factor, " the "It"!

These principles will lead you on the Path of Miracles, to find heavenly riches, rewards, goodness, and blessings here on Earth. Now.

That's the best part. You don't have to wait for it. Why should you? Jesus said, "I have come to give you life and life abundant."[1] He didn't say you have to wait until you die to get it. He didn't say the rewards come only in the afterlife.

---

1 John 10:10 (All references are New Standard Bible unless otherwise noted.)

That abundance exists right here. It's not only in the afterlife. No. No. No. No. No. No *and* no.

Did I emphasize NO?

The fact of the matter is that the Bible says—and these are Jesus's own words to His father, OUR Father— "Thy kingdom come, thy will be done *on Earth* as it is in heaven."[2]

So why do we have to wait to die to live abundantly? Why do we have to wait to die to see God? Why do we have to wait to die to experience full joy? Why do we have to wait to die to live exceedingly, abundantly, above all?

All of these things are waiting for us here. Now.

> *Whatever you want can happen. In this lifetime. Starting now.*

With Christ's resurrection, he guaranteed me eternal life. If I follow him, he said, I am guaranteed that life will go on. That after death, there is life. That my soul will not die. My spirit will continue. That my consciousness and my senses will live forevermore *through* Christ and *in* Christ.

However, that doesn't mean I have to live *in* hell and live *through* hell in order to get to heaven. I can see God's kingdom right here on Earth. I can experience God's love, and His riches, right here.

The seven principles in this book activate heaven so we can live heaven right here. We can experience heaven here on Earth.

Thy kingdom come. On Earth. That's what the Bible says.[3]

These Kingdom Principles will be your guideposts in life. They will help you explain some of the reasons that you have failed, why you haven't been able to get up after you have fallen. But after you adopt them in your life, when you follow them faithfully every day, you *will* be able to get up again, to try again, and to triumph. With them, you won't only find the strength to continue and the will to survive; you'll find the means to succeed.

> *You can experience heaven on Earth, and live exceedingly,*
> *abundantly, above all.*

---

2 Matthew 6:9–13.
3 Matthew 6:10.

They'll make you a spiritual athlete, where you'll see trials as training, instead of as tribulation. You'll draw power from life's tests, energy from its storms, and strength from its challenges.

And every day, you'll find fewer obstacles, fewer hindrances, fewer problems, fewer obstructions, fewer impediments, and fewer difficulties. Because the seven Kingdom Principles change us to such a degree that we're no longer the same. We're better. Life is easier. Things are greater, more abundant. Not just *enough*. Not merely *sufficient*. But exceedingly, abundantly, above all.

I know it myself, in my own life. I've been described as what happens when you put Billy Graham and Martin Luther King Jr. in a blender and put salsa on top. And this book speaks to why I'm here. This is not a sermon for me. I *live* this. This book really defines the principles that led us to the formation of the nation's largest Hispanic Christian organization, to the formation of so many outreach programs and leadership congresses in all fifty states; and to speak out on so many issues, for so many who couldn't speak out for themselves.

Thanks to these principles, I have been able to serve as a conduit and a voice for nearly eighteen thousand evangelical churches and for the sixteen million Hispanic born-again Christians in the United States and Puerto Rico, and to spread God's word on a daily national radio program, a weekly washingtonpost.com blog, and through board advisories on faith and justice issues for the presidential campaigns of both John McCain and Barack Obama.

I grew up in Pennsylvania, the grandson of an Assemblies of God minister, and a devout student of the Bible. But even though I began preaching at the age of fourteen, I didn't discover these principles until later. The Kingdom Principles are simple, powerful, and life-changing, but like so many of God's messages in Scripture, they were woven within the narrative, waiting to be revealed.

And since I discovered them, as I said, my life has changed. As it says in Psalms 119:130, "The unfolding of your words gives light; It gives understanding to the simple."

Just because I'm an evangelical Christian doesn't mean you have to be in order to benefit from these principles. They work for *anyone*, regardless of what church you attend. They can work for you even if you haven't been to church in a while—or even a very long while. You can even be agnostic and say, "This speaks to me."

These principles work for anyone who wants a richer, fuller life, with better friendships, more loving relationships, a more rewarding career, wealth and joy.

The answer to achieving your dreams is here, NOW! Whether you are in a horrible life situation and looking for a way to get out, or you have achieved a measure of success but you know there is even more to be accomplished and attained, these principles are the answer. Whatever you want can happen. In this lifetime. Starting now.

These principles are even for the person who may not know he's searching for an answer. You may not even know that something is missing in your life. But the fact that God put this book in your hands, right now, says something. As you will see in these pages, you may not know what you are looking for in life, you may not know what you are missing—you may not even know that you *are* missing something. But God does. He knows what you are missing, and He knows what you need.

> *God knows what you are missing, and He knows what you need.*

You may just have some vague awareness that *something* is not quite right, that there's something better out there. You may not quite be able to put your finger on it, but you *know.*

Or, you may be fully aware of the fact that there's something missing in your life. It might be that perfect relationship, full of love, sharing, caring, and, yes, passion. It might be that perfect job, that's fulfilling, rewarding, and invigorating; you know—that one where you don't have to drag yourself out of bed to go to work every weekday morning, the one that makes you look forward to Mondays instead of dreading them.

(Do you know that a study published in the *British Medical Journal* found that the risk of heart attack goes up as much as 20 percent as people start the workweek on Mondays? Do you think the people who are having those heart attacks are happy and fulfilled?)

You may have been searching for the answer for a long, long time.

You may have gone bouncing from bad relationship to bad relationship, through breakups or failed marriages, repeating the roles and the heartbreak, wondering why it keeps happening over and over again. You may have quit jobs, changed careers, or resigned yourself to a work life full of drudgery and dissatisfaction. Or you may have felt that every time you were starting to get ahead—or at least catch up—the car or the refrigerator would break down, the kids would need fillings, or you'd get laid off from work and see your bills go soaring all over again.

You may have looked for the answer in other books, and other philosophies—perhaps even other religions.

Look no more. Your search is over.

This is the Path of Miracles.

Chapter 2

THIRD-DAY THINKING

The answer to a new, richer, and fuller life has been available all along, in the best-selling book of all time, the Bible. Specifically, it lies in four short back-to-back chapters describing Christ's resurrection and the days immediately after, until he ascended to heaven to sit at the right hand of the Father.

The account is known (or should be!) by every Christian, for it is the climax of Christ's story, and reveals the great promise awaiting all of his followers: everlasting life in the hereafter.

The story itself is short, simple, and simply told. But it is more than just an account of the resurrection. Within its amazingly brief description of one of the most singularly important events in history is the secret to living a life that is full of God's rewards and riches, fulfillment and abundance—in your relationships, in your job, and in your community. In every area of your life.

Here it is, in a nutshell:

On the third day after Jesus died and was buried, Mary Magdalene went to anoint his body with perfumes. That was the custom, and she didn't even wait for daylight. She ran to the tomb during the night and arrived while it was still dark, just before daybreak. But instead of finding Christ wrapped in the clean linens that were his grave clothes, she found the tomb open and his body gone.

Mary Magdalene ran and told Peter and John, who ran together to see for themselves. When they looked in the empty tomb, they found Christ's grave clothes, the linens he had been wrapped in, neatly folded by the spot where his body had been.

Mary looked in, and she saw two angels sitting there calmly, right where the body was supposed to be. She went out, crying, and met a man she thought was a gardener. It turned out to be Jesus, but she didn't recognize him. He had been transformed.

Later that day, Christ appeared to the disciples in their hideout, the upper room. This room, the upper room, was a special gathering place for them. It was where they shared the Last Supper. And, after Christ appeared to them there, God came rushing in and gave them the power to speak in a language that everyone could understand, no matter where they were from.[1]

The rest, as they say, is history. They went out and spread the word, and Christianity grew—explosively—into the world force that it is today.

Simple. Short. Amazing. The story describes Christ's resurrection, the miracle at the very core of Christianity. It promises us eternal life in the hereafter. But it also contains the lesson of the seven Kingdom Principles:

1. *Life's greatest opportunities arise in our darkest hour.*
2. *Faith and fear always run together.*
3. *God programmed us to have partners.*
4. *There's always an empty tomb right before a filled upper room.*
5. *Order precedes promotion.*
6. *There is transformation, followed by recognition.*
7. *You are assured a filled upper room.*

Mary Magdalene, Peter, and John all ran to the tomb in the dark, before dawn. After day broke, after the sun and the Son had both risen, they recognized the miracle that they had witnessed, and that they had received. But it didn't stop there. It unleashed a marathon of miracles.

> *You can unlock the marathon of miracles in your life.*

The Bible says that in the forty days between his resurrection and when Jesus ascended to heaven, he did so many wondrous things that the world could not hold all the books it would take to describe them all.[2] In other

---

1 John 20, 21; Acts 1, 2.
2 John 21:25.

words, he performed miracle after miracle after miracle—a marathon of miracles.

What happened then can happen now, for you. The Kingdom Principles will lead to your daybreak. They will unlock the marathon of miracles in your life. They will enable you to discover the treasures God has waiting for you, and to live exceedingly, abundantly, above all.

Whatever you ask for, God will give you ten times over, a hundred times over. There's nothing in Scripture that says God answers what we ask for. It says that He answers *exceedingly, abundantly*, above all we could ever imagine or ask for.

If you follow these principles and you pray for a house, you're not going to get a house—you'll get a house with a swimming pool in the backyard and a car out front.

That's the Path of Miracles activation. You change. Your life changes. And the shower of gifts and treasures and blessings begins. If you incorporate these principles into your life, you will receive exceedingly, abundantly, above all.

The primary core, though, is *you*. You no longer apply what I would call First- or Second-Day thinking. You apply Third-Day thinking. You no longer pray for the house; you pray for Him to change you so you can get the house—and then He's not just going to give you the house; He's going to give you the house and the pool and the car and the dog.

Guess what? He already has. It's out there waiting for you.

It's *activation*. That's what it takes. Those things are already there. They exist. They literally exist in the spiritual cosmic reality. In this spiritual domain there is a God who is active, who is involved, but within the parameters of free will.

All we need to do is activate. Turn things on.

And it begins with running in the dark.

PRINCIPLE ONE

LIFE'S GREATEST OPPORTUNITIES ARISE IN OUR DARKEST HOUR

Chapter 3

RUNNING IN THE DARK

I t wasn't a coincidence that it was Peter, John, and Mary Magdalene who ran to the tomb.

Each of them represented a particular narrative in respect to their relationships with Jesus and in respect to their own personal journeys. Each of them had a personal journey that prompted them. I believe wholeheartedly that it wasn't a coincidence that it was Peter, John, and Mary Magdalene who first experienced the reality that the tomb was empty.

We may run together, but we each find what we're each supposed to find.

They were each running for the purpose of finding what they were each missing. It wasn't ambiguous. It wasn't open-ended. It was focused. It was driven. It was specific. They were each looking for something different, and the awesomeness of what they discovered is that they each found what they needed. They each found specifically what they each needed.

Just like us. As we go through our journey, we may run together, but we each find what we're each supposed to find—meaning, when you and your running partner arrive at a specific point together, you find what you're supposed to find and he or she may find something totally different. You find what you need. Others find what they need.

Peter Ran Out of Fear

Peter's relationship with Christ really personifies many of our lives—moments of great faith, moments of great angst; high moments, low moments;

mountains, valleys. It's not a continual upsurge where we personify spiritual growth continuity, where we are so inclined to embracing absolutely everything God has to offer in our lives, where we're continuously positive twenty-four hours a day.

We're reaffirming ourselves—during the course of our day, and during the course of our lives. There's confession, there is a reaffirmation of our families and our relationships.

Our relationship with God tends to be more like that of a ship on a rolling sea: It's full of ups and downs, and we veer off course occasionally, even when we're generally headed in the right direction.

Peter really represents that. It is the same Peter who says, "You are the Christ!"[1]—the reverberating affirmation that is the foundation of the church—and who, in the very next moment, earns the Lord's rebuke: "Satan, get thee behind me."[2]

It's that dichotomy that really speaks to our very existence.

At one moment, we have the greatest amount of faith in ourselves and in God. At the very next moment we find ourselves not believing in God, not believing in ourselves, not believing in our journey, not believing in our purpose.

So, for Peter to be there on the third day, on that morning three days after Christ died and was buried, for Peter to be there running toward that empty tomb, speaks volumes.

> *Peter displays the duality that is in all of us—brave and afraid, faithful and fearful.*

Who's running? It's not just Peter. It's every single human being. It's every single person who has doubted himself. It's every single person who has made some incredible affirmations and commitments and promises and then, the very next day, fell short. It's every single person who had the audacity to actually step out of the boat the way Peter did, to follow Christ and walk across the turbulent waters just as he did; but who then let fear and doubt

---

1 Matthew 16:16; Mark 8:29.
2 Matthew 16:23; Mark 8:33.

shake him and break him and make him falter, just as Peter did, and who then, suddenly, fell in the water.[3]

That's us. And Peter personifies that. He is everyone to whom Jesus can say, "Ye of little faith."[4]

This is the same Peter, of course, who denied knowing Christ to save his own skin. He denied, out of fear.[5] Yet, just before that, the same Peter took out his sword and struck the soldier who came to arrest Christ, Malchus, cutting off his ear.[6] He feared having Jesus taken away by the soldier, taken away from him. His fear caused him to act bravely. As contradictory as it seems, it's not! Peter displays the duality that is in all of us—brave and afraid, faithful and fearful.

So Peter really personifies all humanity. He speaks to our lives in a very clear manner.

And when Peter ran on that day in John, chapter 20, it was faith that ran, but it was also fear. It was strength. It was weakness. It was anxiety and it was security. It was walking on water, and it was falling. It was all that and more. Peter was running in his fear, to face his trepidation and insecurity. That's who ran on that day.

John Ran in Faith

Then we have John. John is the "one whom Jesus loved." John is the one who was always close to Jesus.[7] John, many biblical scholars agree, was one of the youngest of the disciples, undoubtedly, as he's mentioned in Scripture. John represents youthfulness, blind faith, love, the Wow! Factor. John was just awestruck with the ministry and the life of Jesus, and he was the faithful companion.

But I see John from another prism, in the last words of Christ on the cross. He looks at John and he looks at Mary, his mother, and he tells John, "Behold, your mother!" And to Mary he says, "Woman, behold, your son!"[8]

---

3   Matthew 14:29–30.
4   Matthew 6:30, King James Version.
5   Matthew 26:69–75.
6   John 18:10.
7   John 13:23. NAB
8   John 19:26–27.

That tells us, of course, that Jesus viewed John as part of his family.

But it also speaks to another level. He looks at John, and John represents faithfulness. John is that faithful one. John is the one who was always and continuously with him. According to Scripture, wherever Jesus went, John was there. He was the faithful one, the beloved one.

And Mary, the mother of Jesus, represents holiness, virtue, purity, and perseverance.

So what Jesus is really saying is that when holiness and faithfulness are together, when faithfulness takes care of holiness and holiness takes care of fidelity and faithfulness, great things will happen.

John is the beloved. But John's identity was found completely in the life and ministry of Jesus. And when Christ was crucified, John now has this awesome responsibility. Here, for the first time, John runs for himself.

> *John personifies all of us who find ourselves on our own, when we are no longer in the shadow of someone else.*

It's no longer John in the shadow of Jesus. This is just John.

And John, in that moment, on that morning, represents the person discovering that he is on a journey without a guide. That he must find his own way. John is the person, literally and figuratively, in the dark. John is the person asking: "Who am I?" When the most important person in my life, when my mission, when what gave me identity went away—who am I? Who am I when all things are pulled away and I am by myself? I don't have anyone pointing the way for me now. I don't have the PR machinery, and I don't have the marketing campaign. I don't have the infrastructure. It's just me. And it's me alone.

John speaks to loneliness. John speaks to solitude. That's the John who's running that day. The John that day is the one who says, "I'm alone. I've never been alone before, and now I am. For three and a half years I was always in the company of this great master, and now I'm alone. What am I going to do?"

John personifies all of us who find ourselves on our own, discovering our identity. When we are no longer in the shadow of someone else. When that relationship we were a part of is over. When that job that defined us is gone.

When we are all alone, and we're trying to figure out who we are outside of that relationship. When we're trying to figure out who we are, and who we are going to be.

He was running in his loneliness. Just like so many of us.

And he was looking for an answer. Like so many of us.

But here's something many of us could learn from John: Even though he didn't know what the answer would be, his faith told him to keep running until he found it.

When holiness and faithfulness are together, great things will happen.

Chapter 4

MARY MAGDALENE RAN
FOR OTHERS

M ary Magdalene to me really personifies the high point of John 20. This Mary, this woman who was delivered from *seven* spirits according to the biblical narrative.[1]

Here's a side note, to explain what that means.

There are certain numbers that are part of the Jewish narrative of the Talmud and of the Torah that have a special significance: seven, twelve, one hundred twenty, forty—forty days and forty nights; forty years. These are numbers that just resonate from Jewish culture throughout the Hebrew Bible. And, as we know in Scripture, within the Jewish narrative, seven always speaks to completion—the Creation in seven days, and on the seventh he rested. Some would say it's the number of God, because it is the number of completion.

Therefore, in the case of Mary Magdalene, seven spirits means she was completely bound.

On top of that, beginning with Pope Gregory the Great (pope from 590 to 604), church history identifies the Mary Magdalene who ran to the tomb as the same Mary who was somewhat of a harlot.

Now, it's been debated throughout the years as to whether or not the Mary who traveled with Christ and the Mary of ill repute are one and the same, but regardless of whether it was or not, we do know she had seven spirits and that she was delivered from seven spirits. She was completely bound and Jesus freed her.

So here we have Mary Magdalene. It's Mary the failed woman who was

---

1 Luke 8:2.

redeemed. It's Mary the caricature. It's Mary of questionable repute. It's this Mary who runs.

> *When you know what's right, you can't let what others say about you stop you.*

She could have stayed home. She needed to have stayed home. She was a woman of ill repute, a woman with no hope, no destiny. It was ludicrous that she even ran.

But she did. She ran. And she ran while it was still dark.

To me that's the clincher. Biblical scholars all agree that within John's narrative, the time John says this all happened is right before dawn. Right before the sun rises—and we're all aware that it's darkest right before the sun comes up.

So Mary Magdalene ran in the darkest moment. She ran in the darkest hour.

What ignited her? What motivated her? What pushed a woman, a Hebrew woman, to run before the sun rises?

That wasn't a good time for a good Jewish woman to be out. There were specific women who would be out at that time, at what was generally thought to be a bad time, and it was not someone we would call a virtuous character, not someone who would embody what we would call a model example, not an exemplary woman. The women who were out at that hour of the night were, literally and figuratively, women of the night.

But we know that Mary Magdalene—who may or may not have been a woman of the night, and who may or may not have been delivered from those particular spirits—we know for sure she was out, and she was out at the time when good, virtuous women would be at home with their families.

She put all of that aside. She cared not about what others would say. Mary Magdalene cared not at all about the imagery or the repute. She disregarded what the press clippings may have read the next morning or what would be on the cover of the magazines, or what the entertainment shows may have stated about her, or what the blogosphere may have written about her. She ran. She ran while it was still dark, while she had no idea what she was running to.

You have to, too. You can't let what others say about you—or what you *think* they're going to say about you—stop you. When you know your purpose, and you know your goal, you can't let the naysayers or the doubters hold you back. You've got to brush aside the jealous people who don't want others to do better, and ignore the envious people who want to hold others down. When you know what's right, you can't let what others say about you stop you.

But on this day, the third day after Christ was buried: The audacity of that woman! She ran! In the dark.

But not for herself.

> *When we commit ourselves to serving others in their darkest moment, we discover our daybreak.*

This is one of the things I would underline: <u>What made her successful was the fact that she wasn't running for herself</u>. She was running, in essence, to give thanks—the biblical term would be "worship." She was running, of course, to put perfume and scents and fragrances around the body and on the body, as part of the funeral ritual.

But Mary Magdalene ran not for herself. She ran for someone else. She ran to give credit to that person who took her out of her miring clay, who took her out of her difficult circumstance. She ran to acknowledge others who had blessed her throughout her life. Who had equipped her. Who had been there throughout her journey.

Jesus died, but inside herself, she was dying. Because the only person who ever acknowledged and affirmed her, who gave her value and took her out, her deliverer, her purpose in living, was gone.

She's what? An obscure woman? Of ill repute? Of questionable repute in the best-case scenario. And then along came this man, Jesus, and this woman, this possible prostitute, this bottom-of-the-barrel woman, all of a sudden gains incredible media attention. It would be the equivalent today of having a prostitute or a homeless person and taking them and putting them overnight in the president's cabinet, overnight on the team of someone out there who's really transforming things. It's incredible to think about.

And then he dies.

So the question is, does she go back to a life of prostitution? Will she go back now? Will she go back to the seven spirits who bound her, whatever those were? Will she digress back to her miring clay? Will she go back to her life without value and identity and clarity? To her oppression?

These are the questions surrounding Mary Magdalene on that fateful morning. In the darkest part of the night, in those black hours before dawn. The light that had come into her life and lifted her up was gone, and, as she ran to put the scents and fragrances on Christ's body, she was surrounded by so many questions.

Still, regardless of all of that, she ran to serve someone else, in his darkest moment.

> *We may find our daybreak at a time when we take our personal darkness and we shift it aside.*

This woman was basically saying, "Regardless of how difficult my day may be, regardless of how dark it may be, there is someone else who is experiencing an even darker moment. And my job is to somehow alleviate that darkness.

"I'm going to go into this tomb, to this man who is so important in my life, who is now dead, and I'm going to acknowledge him and I'm going to serve him."

Mary Magdalene ran to worship this man, to put fragrances and scents on him. And that is the key. That speaks to the opportunity of finding my daybreak when I serve someone else in his most difficult time of need.

Many times in our lives, when we commit ourselves to serving someone else in their darkest moment, we actually discover our daybreak. Just like Mary Magdalene. Our daybreak may come not when we have tunnel vision and focus ourselves entirely, exclusively on our own darkness and our own circumstance. When we're experiencing our hell and when we have that great mountain, that great obstacle before us, our secret of success and our breakthrough may come when we don't focus on that mountain, but we focus on someone else's mountain and try with every fabric of our being to serve and get that person out first. We may find our daybreak at a time when we take our personal darkness and we shift it aside.

> *If I can help those around me come out of their darkest moment,*
> *in doing so I will come out of mine*

When I experience my darkness in life, whenever these dark moments come and they get darker and darker, the very first thing I do is not ask, "How can I get out of this?" The very first thing I do is look around to see who's going through a similar moment, and say, "Let me serve them."

If I can help my brother and my sister, if I can help those around me come out of their darkest moment, in doing so I will come out of mine. If I serve them in their darkest moment I can find my daybreak—even when I think I have nothing to give, when I encourage when I have no courage, when I give hope when I'm hopeless.

I know that sounds oxymoronic—how can you give something that you don't have?

Because it may not be something that you *have*, it may be something that you *are*. Meaning, your very life gives hope. Your very presence. You may not have it embedded inside you, it may not be something you carry with you, but it's part of who you are. Your very life gives hope regardless of what you can do. Your very life is hope in a package. It's embodied hope. Our Spiritual DNA, how God created us, we are hope. We are faith for someone. We are love to someone. We are mercy and justice to someone. Justice is not something that we do, it's who we are.

And in our darkest hour, we can still give hope to someone else.

Chapter 5

THE FAITH OF GOD

Let's talk a little bit about faith. Let's talk a little bit more about John.

We paid an awful lot of attention to Peter, and it's true that fear can be an overwhelming force in all of our lives. It can be the thing that prevents us from moving, it can be the thing that blinds us to the direction we should run in, and it is also that impetus that leads us to run.

But faith guides us. Faith supports us. Faith not only guides us and supports us, faith will protect all the things that are pure.

Let's go back to the crucifixion and Jesus. Remember the words of Christ on the cross as he instructs John, the beloved, "Behold, your mother!"[1] Faith takes care of the things that are pure in our lives. Of the innocent. The untouched. The unashamed. Faith protects that.

So faith provides hope.[2] Faith sees things that we cannot see.[3] Faith facilitates the avenue of transformation. Faith dances when fear will weep.

> *We don't just have faith in God; we have the faith of God.*

Faith, of course, will see the cup half filled. But, to be honest, I'm looking at a faith that sees the cup exceedingly, abundantly, running over. Normal faith, common faith—for lack of a better term, human faith—sees the cup half filled. Human faith gives us a positive outlook. Human faith helps us look forward to a brighter tomorrow.

---

1   John 19:26–27.
2   1 Corinthians 13:13.
3   Hebrews 11:1.

But—pay attention to this! Here's a notion that I want you to understand—this is not *our* faith.

Never in Scripture, never in the Bible is there anything that's written about *our* faith. From the apostle Paul[4] to Peter[5] and John[6] it reads: "the faith *of* God."

We already have that faith gene in us. It is not a "my faith" or "your faith." It is God's faith. God equipped us with faith. He transferred his DNA to me. And that's what makes me believe when others would say there is no chance and there is no hope.

My mom to this day will remember walking into my room and being very concerned about her five-year-old boy lying on the ground praying. Because we were members of a Pentecostal church and that's not something they did in the Pentecostal church. It was always on your knees. And there I was, praying out loud.

My mom just recently reminded me that she thought I had some serious psychological issues. She said it wasn't normal for a five-year-old boy to be so committed to prayer. But there I was, five years old, praying every day. I was attracted by the idea of an all-powerful, Almighty God. I was attracted to the idea that there was somebody out there and that they would listen to me.

Really, until I was about seven or eight years old, I would literally walk to the bus stop talking, moving my lips, because I was praying. Because no one ever told me that if someone saw me praying as I was walking they would think I was talking to myself. To me, God existed; I want to talk to him, and okay, why not?

So it wasn't until I was seven or eight years old and my sister was accompanying me one day and she said, "What are you doing?"

I said, "I'm praying."

She said, "Do you know you're moving your lips?"

I said, "Okay, because I'm talking to God."

And then she said, "Yeah, but listen: People don't understand that. And they're going to think you're cuckoo."

That was the first time I woke up to the reality that not everybody talks to God. I thought God had a conversation with everyone. I really felt God's

---

4   Acts 14:27.
5   2 Peter 1:1–3.
6   John 5:4.

presence. I knew God was there, and He would listen. Because I had the faith of God in me. We all do.

We don't just have faith *in* God, we have the faith *of* God.

And it is through that faith, through that prism, through those lenses, that I see my world. Through the faith of God I see a better day when everyone else says there's absolutely no way we can change the world. Through the faith of God and through the prism of His eyes I see that, in fact, we can change it—for good.

His faith is the condition of things hopeful and the assurance of things not seen.[7] His faith is the prism by which I view my world, and it shapes how I see the world and how I see my life and my surroundings, and how I see God.

Faith acts as the lens through which I see God, my community, my family, my surroundings, my circumstances, and myself. I'm using His lenses, His glasses.

That's pretty incredible. Because it's the faith of God that helps me see not just the way the world is, but the way it can be.

> *The faith of God helps me see not just the way the world is, but the way it can be.*

It's going to take action. It's definitely going to take action. I connect it with the work, because faith without works is dead.[8] That's what it says in the Bible. Faith without works is useless.[9] Faith without works is dead.

But by His faith and my action, I can help the world change. I can see my community change. I can see that marriage change and that relationship restored. I can see that business turn around.

Except, it's not my faith that does it, it's the faith of God.

All I need to do is activate it.

---

7   Hebrews 11:1.
8   James 2:26.
9   James 2:20.

Chapter 6

THE MAGNITUDE OF
YOUR COMING GLORY

Mary Magdalene was the first to reach the tomb.

Think about it: Mary Magdalene, a woman. The first one to ever experience the fullness of the secret, to witness the miracle of the resurrection, was a woman.

Now, those who are familiar with the Adam and Eve story in the Garden of Eden, whether they read it literally or as a metaphor, regardless, the fact of the matter is that we see in that story that it was a woman who first fell into the trap.

All of a sudden, with Mary Magdalene, this story comes full circle!

It's as if God said, "Listen, I'm going to provide this opportunity for you to totally redeem yourself. I'm not only going to redeem you in your personal experience, in your personal journey, but I have the power to redeem the entire story. I have the power to fix the narrative. I have the power to contextualize your journey in a way that will make you understand that what you went through was *with* a purpose and *for* a purpose. That even the negative things that we go through in life speak to the positive things we experience, and they're totally connected."

It's as if God is saying, "You can measure the magnitude of your upcoming blessing by the measure of the hell that you've been through in life."

> *You can measure the magnitude of your upcoming blessing by the measure of the hell that you've been through in life.*

What you went through in your life was for a purpose. You can measure the magnitude of the coming glory, of the coming abundance, of everything marvelous that is coming your way by the measure of the hell you have gone through. It is directly proportional.

We can measure what's coming according to what we went through. We are going to be blessed according to what we went through. In theological terms, we will be *anointed* according to where we are going. Which means we are going to be prepared and equipped according to where we are going. We will be blessed according to what we went through, but we will be equipped and anointed according to where we are going.

So we can't lose hope, and we can't lose faith, because that darkness, that moment in the abyss, is telling us how wonderful the future is for us.

Embrace the night. Embrace it. It seems a bit masochistic to a degree, but it isn't. John of the Cross, the noted Catholic mystic and author of *The Dark Night of the Soul*, said the darkness leads to an even greater illumination and union with God. In other words, it leads to daybreak. The night speaks to the day. That confrontation, that negative moment, that loss of a relative, however hard and arduous it may be, however difficult it may be in the moment, it speaks to what is to come when the sun rises. And, again, it is directly proportional.

> *We can't lose hope, and we can't lose faith, because that moment in the abyss is telling us how wonderful the future is for us.*

I can look at my darkest moment with hope, because I know that the more I'm going through the greater my reward will be. It's directly proportional. It really is.

As I suffer I know that if I can hold on and get through this, if I don't give up, my reward will be proportional to the pain I felt.

I'll relate it to a Scriptural narrative and through a life application.

Everybody knows the great story of David and Goliath—how David, a little shepherd boy armed with nothing but a simple sling, slew the giant.[1]

Twice a day for forty days (there's one of those significant Scriptural numbers again!), Goliath had challenged the Israelites to send out their champion to face him. But the king and his men were afraid. Understandably.

---

1 1 Samuel 17:1–58.

Who wouldn't be? I mean, Goliath is a giant! He's huge and fierce. And David, this young man, armed with nothing but a sling and five stones—he doesn't even wear any armor—stands up to him.

Naturally, after David wins, the king makes him commander of his army. And from there, it's only a matter of time before David becomes king himself.

But what does this story tell us today? It's not just that Goliath was a giant and David was brave. It speaks to the fact that this giant arises in order to usurp, in order to prevent David from seeing the other side. The giant is this great opponent of a person in front of him. And by slaying the giant David then became king.

Sure, there were some hurdles along the way, but eventually David became king. From the moment he took charge and cast that stone, his destiny was set in motion. He stepped up to the plate and decided his fate.

My point is, the greater the obstacle that arises before you speaks to the greatness of what God has for you. If we would embrace this idea, then it would motivate us and encourage us to run in the dark.

Whatever it may be—if it's an addiction that needs to be overcome, if it is some sort of infirmity or sickness, if it is an obstacle at work in your career, an accident, a death, whatever it may be—it speaks directly to the size of what's to come. You can literally measure the size of what's coming according to what you go through. And it's directly proportional.

> *The greater the obstacle that arises before you speaks to the greatness of what God has for you.*

Chapter 7

FINDING PURPOSE IN TRAGEDY

The greatest tragedy, it is said, is to lose a child. The younger the child is, the more tragic it is.

I met a man at one of our conferences who lost his daughter. She was a teenager, an innocent victim killed by a drunk driver. Imagine the pain that those parents suffered when they lost that child.

How can we ever justify that? How can we ever contextualize that within this framework?

Well, here's what happened in the case of those parents, who lost that daughter to that drunk driver: After that, these parents committed themselves. After that, they understood that their calling was to raise incredible awareness and disdain for drunk driving.

> *Every single tragedy and obstacle we face speaks to the blessings and to the glory and to the greatness we will experience.*

We know, of course, the story of Mothers Against Drunk Drivers (MADD). But I speak to another story. These parents committed themselves to going to every high school and re-creating a drunk driving accident scene in order to really impact the hearts of these young people, to imprint indelibly in their minds the need to be very cautious, to not drink and drive.

In city after city, they played out these scenes, complete with smashed cars and bloody victims. They used students from the school they were at as actors, and spattered them with fake blood, which made it all the more vivid because they were people the other students actually knew.

Then they created the metrics where for several years after they made their presentation they would come back to the schools and see the number of DUIs and the number of accidents and tragedies coming from the graduates of those schools—and they all dramatically decreased. Among the students and the graduates of the schools where they made their demonstrations there were significantly fewer drunk driving incidents than there were among students and graduates at other schools.

In this way, those parents—who had suffered so much, lost the most precious thing a parent could lose—understood that behind the tragedy there was this unbelievable daybreak that enabled them to do greater good.

That really fulfilled them. They saw the spirit of their daughter embedded in every single presentation and they saw the spirit of their daughter disseminate through the acts of charity and awareness. They saw the spirit of their daughter save the lives of so many other sons and daughters, and keep other parents from suffering the way they had.

> *What you went through in your life was for a purpose.*

Every single tragedy and obstacle we face speaks to the blessings and to the glory and to the greatness we will experience if only we have the wherewithal to run while it's still dark. To run when we have no idea where we're going. Mary Magdalene, Peter, and John ran in the darkness just before dawn, after losing the most important person in their lives—and they found the amazing miracle of Christ's resurrection.

Chapter 8

THE TEMPERING OF THE SWORD

Our dark moments, the trials we face in life, the challenges and tribulations that assail us, serve a purpose. They speak to the glory of what is to come, but they also prepare us and strengthen us right now.

We all know that in the making of a sword, the blacksmith puts it through a process of heating and cooling and hammering and reheating—over and over again—to harden and temper the steel. It is long and laborious work, but the more painstaking the effort, the stronger the sword.

That is what our dark moments do for us. To take the metaphor further: life is the anvil and God is the blacksmith. And the tests, the tragedies, and the travails are the hammer.

Instead of thinking of the pounding as punishment, we should realize it is part of the process of making us better, and stronger. You have to temper the steel so that it can stand up to the task. It prepares us to go forth and face our enemies and cut away the obstacles in our way.

And, just as with the sword, the longer the pounding lasts and the harder it is, the better and stronger we will be when it's finished. It's that proportional thing again—the outcome will be directly in keeping with what we go through.

Here's another way of looking at it:

No pain, no gain.

How many times have you heard that?

It's true. Olympic athletes, professional sports stars, and the very best college contenders know it. They know that you can't become the best you can be if you don't keep going, training, running, and pushing when it hurts. If you quit, you can't compete.

It's just that simple. You have to keep running. If you're going to go to the Olympics, you don't do it just because you think you're going to go to the Olympics. You've got to get out and do what it takes to make it. You have to sweat, and strain, and give it your all, even when you think you have nothing left to give—especially when you think you have nothing left to give. You've got to try as hard as you can today, then try even harder tomorrow.

> *If you quit, you can never reach your goal.*

Those athletes are tempering their bodies, the same way the blacksmith tempers the sword.

And they know that there are many, many, many days when it will seem hopeless. They know that there are many, many, many times when they're going to think the pain is just not worth it, that they're never going to reach their goal, that they're just not good enough.

But they also know that if they quit, they lose. If you quit, you can never reach your goal. Never. You have to keep running. You have to keep trying.

It's true for athletes. It's true for actors. It's true for you.

It's true of the great thinkers, those men and women whose ideas have changed the world. Do you think Einstein just fell out of bed and dashed off the theory of relativity one Saturday morning? It's true of the great entrepreneurs and businessmen who had so many failures before that one idea clicked. It's said that Edison tried more than a thousand times before he made the first lightbulb that stayed lit.

They all had their dark moments. They all had their "I want to give up" moments. They all went through a darkest hour, a time when they thought they just couldn't take it anymore, that it just wasn't worth it, that God wasn't on their side.

Jewel Kilcher, the singer best known by her first name, is a perfect example. She grew up in a house in Alaska with no indoor plumbing—in the 1980s. At one point she was so poor she lived in a van and sang for change on the street. But she was determined. She didn't give up. And before she even turned twenty-one, her debut album came out and became one of the best-selling first albums of all time.

Yet we look at all of these people and we think they led charmed lives. We think that they haven't gone through things or aren't going through things just because we see their outward success.

Behind that appearance of success they may be going through that great moment of darkness. Behind a lot of these personal narratives of success, there is pain and suffering, trials and tribulations.

The vast majority of successful people—be it the stars we see, those of us whom we see in certain levels of power in industry and finance—they've all been through the dark, dark, dark, dark, dark moment—the "dark nights of the soul," as the Catholic writer John of the Cross called them. And when I say dark, I mean to the extreme. Some may still be. For some of them, the outer façade may be just that—a façade, which is really covering up a continuing darkness. Some of them have yet to experience a daybreak. No matter what it looks like from the outside.

Imagine how much richer their lives would be if they did experience a daybreak. They're already successful, by most earthly standards. What does God have in store for them that they have yet to realize? When they feel the true joy and grace that He has for each and every one of us? What then?

> *The outcome will be directly in keeping with what we go through.*

There are those stories you hear where it happened by chance—people who've won giant lottery prizes, or the factory workers who pitched in together in a lottery pool and won big. That's the anomaly.

And, more often than we realize, their victory is short-lived. It's a taste of what could be if they were willing to run harder, to face their fears, to help others. It's an opportunity for them to show they will do more than talk about doing the right thing; it's a chance for them to truly help others.

That doesn't mean they should have given their money away. But they could have taken that money and started a charitable foundation, or used it as seed money for a company that makes something people really need. Instead, they quit their jobs, go on a cruise around the world, buy a big house and a fancy car. And in a few years, they're broke. Right back where they started.

Which do you think God wanted?

I think God gave them an opportunity, and they blew it. They quit running. They saw that win as the end, instead of as a means to an end. They saw it as the finish line, instead of as a starting line for something even greater.

Chapter 9

MAKING THE MOST OF THE STORM

Good people hide when the storm arrives, but great people rise up and take advantage of the storm to thrive and catapult them to their destiny. Good people see a problem; great people see an opportunity. That's why, when the storm arises, good people will hide. Great people will thrive. Great people say, "This is my opportunity."

From the fisherman's perspective, by the way, it is without a doubt a reality. Coming from Pennsylvania, I'm privy to some of that. I did a lot of work in Boston and New England, with some of the lobster and crab fishermen from New England. And it's amazing how, before the storm, in the calmness preceding the rising wind and churning waves, it's precision. It's a good catch.

But the greatest catch comes when? When the swells arrive. When the storm comes. That's accepted. It's risky, isn't it? But the rewards come when people are willing to take risks.

> *Good people see a problem; great people see an opportunity.*

That doesn't mean taking foolish risks. That doesn't mean wishing you could fly and jumping off a building. It doesn't mean quitting your job to go start a business of your own without doing the preparation. The fishermen know what they're doing. They're experts. They're prepared. And it's still risky!

There was a movie with George Clooney a few years back, *The Perfect Storm*, that told the story of these fishermen fighting to get a big catch. The movie, by the way, is based on a true story. They knew that the greatest catch would occur when the waves were impacting the boat. When the sea was raging. When there were clouds and thunder. That when the storm arose they could actually have their greatest catch.

It's risky—as we saw in the movie. You may lose your life in the process, and they did. But there are very few people who understand that in the darkest moment, when the storm arises, you can actually achieve some of life's greatest outcomes and some of life's greatest achievements. You can come out not just alive and well, but victorious.

And I don't mean you have to risk your life. I'm not saying you should put your life on the line. I'm saying that this thing of hiding until the storm goes away does not necessarily speak to our DNA. *We were created to confront the storm.* We were created to thrive in the midst of that storm.

There are so many examples in the business world and in personal applications of people who, in the midst of their most difficult hour, kept trying, and came out champions.

> *In the darkest moment, when the storm arises, you can actually achieve some of life's greatest outcomes and some of life's greatest achievements.*

It is the Lance Armstrongs of the world who truly understand what it means to keep trying in their darkest hour. Armstrong is the only man to win the grueling twenty-three-day Tour de France seven times. Seven! In a row! One right after the other.

And, as incredible as that is, all seven of his victories came *after* he was diagnosed with testicular cancer—which had spread to his lungs *and* his brain—and underwent lengthy surgery and drug regimen to beat it. Most would have been happy simply to survive. Not Armstrong. In the midst of that cancer his mind was already on the next Tour de France. Not only did he overcome the cancer, he was victorious.

Most people who found out they had cancer would give up the racing. Many would have given up living. Many would have wallowed, and cried, and cursed the heavens. Some might even curse God. The first thought, often enough, is: "God, why did you do this to me?"

That's the thinking of people who don't know how to run in the dark, to keep trying in their most difficult time, and seize the energy of the storm. They think the Good Lord has given them cancer out of some vindictiveness, or as punishment for something they did wrong.

But let's look closely at Lance Armstrong's story. He got cancer, and kept going. He beat the cancer and won the Tour de France—the toughest race in bicycling—*seven* times. And here's the incredible part: A medical research article published in the journal *Medical Hypothesis* in 2006 proposed that *the cancer might have actually helped him win*. The report suggested that Armstrong's hormone levels changed as a result of the cancer surgery, and boosted his performance.

Talk about God working in mysterious ways!

But it was still up to Lance Armstrong to keep riding, to keep training, to keep trying, to not give up. God didn't ride that bicycle over the mountains of France. He might have been right there next to Armstrong the whole way, but Lance Armstrong was the one who had to keep pedaling.

It's those types of stories that prove that in the most difficult moment, you let that difficult moment serve as the impetus of confrontation and success. That you can thrive in the midst of the most difficult moment. That you can sail through the storm and you can use it to your advantage.

> *Use the momentum that comes against you to catapult you toward your next destiny.*

Let's put it another way.

It's about energy. The storm has greater energy than the calm. By the very nature of the activity, the storm has greater energy than calm seas—the friction, the amount of kinetic energy, the built-up potential energy, all that energy! It's much greater than when things are not churning, when they're still.

Why not channel that energy? Why not utilize that energy as a platform that catapults you toward your next dimension?

That's what we need to do. We need to take the energy of the storm and, instead of hiding from it, find a way in our lives to channel it. Let's capture the energy of the storm. Let's capture the thrust.

In self-defense, in martial arts, you learn to use the attack, the assault and the energy of he who comes before you against the attacker. To use the momentum.

Well, that's what we should do in life: Use the momentum that comes against you—channel it, harness it, and use it as a platform to catapult you toward your next destiny.

Chapter 10

BRICKS WITHOUT STRAW

We all know the story of Moses and the Hebrews enslaved in Egypt.[1]

The Hebrews were forced to work as laborers for their Egyptian masters, constructing massive building projects under orders from Pharaoh. It was difficult and grueling work, making and moving loads of bricks under the blazing sun in the heat of the Egyptian desert.

The Hebrews had to make the bricks themselves, mixing mud and straw. Hard as that was, though, after Moses asked Pharaoh to give the Hebrews time off to worship, it got worse. Pharaoh was so upset with them that he took away the straw and he basically said, "It's time to make bricks without straw."[2]

Now that's pretty outrageous. That will multiply the work. That will make it more difficult. How can you structure the mortar and clay into bricks without the straw that basically served as the strengthening mechanism in the brick? It's going to be putty.

So Pharaoh said, "I'm going to take away one of your primary ingredients, the straw. Now you're going to have to make bricks without straw."

In life, sometimes we are called to make bricks without straw. We are challenged to continue to build our lives, even when all the resources are not there. Sometimes we are called to build even when we lose that person we love so much or have emptiness in our heart, when we don't have the financial wherewithal or we don't have the support mechanisms. Or we don't believe in ourselves. We're told to keep going anyway. We have to build without straw. We have to continue to construct our lives.

What do we do?

---

1   Exodus 2–40.
2   Exodus 5:7.

Well, the Hebrews continued to build. It was more difficult, but they continued to build.

And look at what the reward was: The reward was that Pharaoh finally released them. All the plagues set in and he said, I can't take this anymore, and he set them free.

And this is what the Bible said that I think is just so astonishing:

The Bible said that the Egyptian people gave the Hebrew children their riches, their gold, their dresses.

So we have a bunch of former slaves who go off walking in the desert, looking like Fifth Avenue.

Why? Because they continued to build when they should not have. Because in the midst of the most difficult storm, they thrived. Because they laid bricks without straw.

And, once again, here we have one of those laws: the reward exceeded the confrontation, the struggle, the pain, the angst.

In life, sometimes we are called to make bricks without straw.

They stuck with it, even when they didn't have the proper resources. They kept trying, and doing what was necessary, even though one of the primary ingredients for them to succeed had been taken away.

Do you do that? Do you keep going when it seems impossible for you to succeed? Or do you give up?

It's easy to quit. It's easy to say, "That's enough; it can't be done." The hard part is to keep going, against all odds. The hard part is to look at the challenge as an opportunity—to say, "I don't have that anymore. What *will* work? How can I make this work?"

Necessity, they say, is the mother of invention. When people need something badly enough, they come up with a solution. Well, I'm here to tell you that sometimes, God gives us a challenge so that we can come up with something new. Your path to success may be through that challenge, and God knows that the only way for you to realize that is for Him to put that obstacle in your way.

Otherwise, why would you? If things are working fine, most people just keep doing things the way they are. God knows you may believe that old saying—"If it ain't broke, don't fix it."

But what if it can be done better? Will you make the world a better place without feeling that something is broken? Will you build a better mousetrap if the one you have works just fine? If you will, then that's not where God is going to put the challenge in your life. The challenge is going to come in the area where you need it most. The challenge is going to come in the area you need to improve, or in the area you are meant to improve for the rest of us.

Or, sometimes, as happened with the Hebrews and the bricks, the purpose of the challenge won't be obvious. The challenge won't seem directly related to the reward. But, make no mistake about it—it's no accident. Everything happens for a reason.

Chapter 11

THINGS ARE ALREADY
SET IN MOTION

The reason the sun rises right after the darkest moment of the night is because the world revolves on its own—things have already been set in motion. Through natural laws and the laws of physics, through God's creation, things have been set in motion.

At congresses that I participate in across the country, I actually bring out a globe and I spin the globe and I say, "Listen, this is planet Earth on its axis, and here are the Newtonian principles—the law of inertia, the law of opposite and equal returns."

As I explain in those gatherings, the reason the earth is still spinning, regardless of the meteorites and comets, regardless of the objects from outer space that have hit this planet—and we're privy to the fact that they have hit the planet, you can ask a couple of dinosaurs who are no longer with us—is because it has been set in motion. Therefore, it continues in motion.

There are plenty of craters that are indicative of the fact this planet has been bombarded throughout its history. However, it continues to spin because it has been set in motion. Once God got it going, it keeps going.

Your life is just the same. Once God starts things in your life, once God says, "Yes, go!" you keep going. You're still in motion, regardless of the comets and meteorites and things that have hit you.

Your appearance may change. You may go through an ice age. Your surroundings may change, and so may some of the people you surround yourself with. However, you'll still be set in motion.

Things are set in motion in your life even before you get here. I'll show you what I mean.

Years after I was involved in ministry, my father told me a story.

"When I was fourteen years old," he said, "I walked into church one day with no intentions at all of having any kind of spiritual experience. I went in there, to be honest, because I had a girl I was trying to date."

My father, clearly, was not the most spiritually committed young person in Christianity. He had one interest in mind and that was that blue-eyed girl. But he went in church that day looking for her, and a visiting woman missionary he had never seen before called out to him.

"You! Come here!" she said.

We're Disciples of Christ, we're mainline Christians. But my father's church in Puerto Rico had gotten into the renewal charismatic movement and believed that God could speak through them. (The prophetic voice may actually be legitimate, even today. The Word of God speaks to us through people.)

"I don't know you," that woman missionary said, "but all I know is that out of you, out of your loins shall come a voice that I, the Lord, have sent, that I will use for my glory, and I will do great things with. And it's going to be such a powerful voice, and so many lives are going to be changed by that voice that I'm going to protect you throughout your journey, because of that voice that will come out of you."

And my dad told me, "I was fourteen years old and I had no idea what she was talking about. I just walked out of there going, 'This is just not normal.'"

The years passed, he said, "And I had no idea what she was talking about until I saw you pick up the microphone for the first time." Then, he said, "I got it."

For my dad, that was proof that things are already set in motion, both the good and the bad.

> ### We have to let the faith happen.

When dark times come, they will be followed by a daybreak. The tragedies and conflicts and difficult moments that we face in our lives speak to the goodness and the greatness and the fullness of what we are about to experience. All we need to do is hold on and have the audacity to run in the dark.

We don't worry when we see the sun go down at night. We know it will rise again. When the darkness settles down upon the earth, we don't panic. We don't just quit. We don't just curl up in a ball on the floor and whimper. We have faith that the light will return in the morning, and that the sun's warmth will chase away the chill of the night. We know morning will come and the dark time will be gone.

That faith is quintessentially important. God already set things in motion, and He put the faith element in it. There's nothing that can stop it but God.

We know that. But for some silly reason, we can have faith about the larger things, but not about our own lives. We know the sun will come up in the morning. We know the tide that goes out will come back in. We know that winter will be followed by spring.

But we ignore those things in our own lives. We don't put on His glasses. We close our eyes to faith and we let fear blind us. We lose hope.

What we have to do is let that faith happen. We have to allow that faith to happen. We have to let the faith of God flow through us.

We do that by continuing to run in the dark, with fear at our side. Sometimes we even have to run directly *at* fear, to our moment of solitude, which becomes our moment of confrontation, which leads to revelation. It leads to the moment when I discover that everything is already waiting for me. It leads to the moment when I discover that He already took care of my path, when I realize that everything was indeed already set in motion, and when I discover that my future is likewise in His hands.

But I have choices. Even though things have been set in motion by Him, and my future is in His hands, I have choices. It's that free will thing again: I can run away from the tomb or I can run to it. I can run in the dark, or I can give up and stay locked up in my room.

If we give up, we don't reach the daybreak. If we stay home and refuse to run we're never going to experience the second half. If we run, we leave the dark times behind and find our daybreak. If we fall down, we have to get back up again.

We have to keep running. That's how we arrive at the dawn.

Chapter 12

PREPARE FOR DAYBREAK

It is those who run through the darkness first who find the dawn first. While others are sleeping. While others are in their own comfortable modality. While others are complacent. While others are satisfied. The ones who run through the darkness find the daybreak.

What does the Bible tell us? "Awaken from sleep; for now salvation is nearer to us than when we believed. The night is almost gone, and the day is near."[1]

This is our great wake-up call. It truly is. I believe the vast majority of us spend our lives sleeping. Not literally. Not lying in bed snoring. But metaphorically. We spend our lives with our eyes closed. We spend our lives oblivious to what is going on around us. And, even when we dream, we don't get up and make those dreams come true.

The vast majority of us work and live and look forward to the sleep. It should be the other way around. It *has* to be the other way around.

We should sleep in order to look forward to the day. We should use our sleep to recharge our batteries—to renew our bodies, refresh our minds, and revitalize our souls—so that we can charge into the new day ready to make our dreams come true. We should open our eyes and seize the day. We should look for opportunities to make ourselves better people, and the world a better place. We should go out energized and ready to do His will, to build a Kingdom Culture here, and to create heaven on Earth.

Imagine if people truly wake up, what we can do.

> *When you run through the darkness, you find the dawn.*

---

1   Romans 13:11–12.

The opportunity lies in that great shift between the darkest moments and dawn. The opportunity comes when you run when everyone else refuses to. When you run in spite of the criticism, in spite of the different obstacles and hindrances. It's when you really, truly wake up and say, "This is my day. And I will be there first."

Let's not forget that the dawn and the darkness connect yesterday and tomorrow. I want to be there at the crevice of growth. I want to be there with the capacity and the wherewithal to be the first one to say good-bye to my yesterday, and be the first one to say hello to my tomorrow.

If I run through the darkness, and I don't give up and I don't ask God to change my circumstances but, instead, I ask Him to make me a better me so that I can go out and make my world a better place, I will find the dawn. I will not just be rewarded; I will be lavished with gifts.

And God does it one better. He doesn't make you wait all the way to the end to be rewarded. The reward occurs even in the running itself! The running in itself is a reward. Running toward that empty place, running with all things coming against you. You will never, ever, ever, ever go through a difficult moment in your life without walking out richer.

You apply these principles and you adhere to them and you assimilate them and they become part of your DNA. Every single journey that you go through, you will walk out richer. There will never be a "Why did I have to go through this kind of experience?" You *will* walk out richer. And the reward will be exceedingly, abundantly, above all we ever asked for. It will be exceedingly, abundantly, above all we could ever imagine.

> *You will never, ever go through a difficult moment in your life without walking out richer.*

The tests and challenges in our life are God-ordained. That's not some sort of theology of pseudomasochism or of suffering. It is the reality of mankind. It is the reality of our personal journeys. It is a process.

We live in a process universe, and we live in a process world, and we live in a process spiritual reality. And by process I mean we cannot jump one stage over the other; we *must* go through stages. From our infancy to our toddler years and our youth to adulthood—all the way from the cradle to the grave—we go through stages.

It's a growth, a maturation of who and what we are. There also is a spiritual growth in what we experience in our lives, and it is in that process where darkness precedes dawn. It is ordained. There is a purpose. And it is a sign. The old saying is true: it *is* darkest before the dawn. So when things are at their darkest, my great acclamation and my great callout would be: "Prepare for daybreak!"

We all face those dark moments. You can't escape them. They're there. It's inevitable. But after the darkness comes the dawn. Always. And the sense in my heart is that through Scripture and through our journey that what the Lord is telling us is to prepare for daybreak, particularly in those dark moments in our lives.

Life's greatest opportunities arise in our darkest hour. That's hard to believe, I know. It's hard to accept when you're in the depths of your darkness, when the waves are pounding and you think you're drowning, and you can't see the shore.

But Mary Magdalene, Peter, and John ran in the darkest hour and discovered the miracle of the resurrection. They received something they never expected, something greater than they could have imagined, by running through the darkest of times.

Do you think you can even begin to imagine the miracle waiting for you?

> *Life's greatest opportunities arise in our darkest hour.*

The vast majority of human beings never experience fullness. And what I mean by fullness is that they never fully experience what God intended for their lives to be—the full picture. What I would call the Wow! Factor in life. Not the survivability, but the success of life. And not just earthly success, not success by the metrics of the world—we're not just speaking of financial success and measurable outcomes depicted by material wealth and gain. I speak to success of heart.

Those measurable, material outcomes can play into it. Sure, absolutely—as a good businessman, as an entrepreneur, being whatever you may be. But more important, finding success in your family, in your home, in your relationships, in your marriage, in your own person. Through your children. Through your children's children. That level of: "I've reached it!" Or, if you haven't reached it yet, knowing full well, "I'm on my way."

That level of fulfillment. That's success of heart.

And it's all when we prepare ourselves for daybreak. It's all when we understand that in this process there is darkness, and darkness will come. But we've been set in motion. And because we've been set in motion, we are guaranteed a daybreak.

Chapter 13

MAKING CHOICES, FINDING THE PATH

We all have the same choices as Mary Magdalene: We can stand in the midst of condemnation or run in the shelter of grace. We can stand in the midst of our failures and sins or we can run under the canopy of righteousness and mercy.

Our life is about the choices we make. Every single day we make choices. And the outcome of the day is based on the choices we make that day. It is that free will component that distinguishes us from the animal kingdom.

Choices.

Mary Magdalene had choices. Mary Magdalene had alternatives. Mary Magdalene had some options. Her primary option was to stay right where she was. She could have stood in her past. She could have not moved, not taken responsibility, not run. Yet she was propelled, she was driven to run toward Grace.

What drove her? What picked her up that morning? What was her incentive?

Her incentive was, first and foremost, redemption. She had experienced what it is to be changed, what it is to be loved and embraced when no one else embraced her, with purity and honesty and virtue. She was driven by that. She was driven by purity.

We are driven to pure things. We are driven to transparent things. We are driven to transparent people. To transparent relationships. To transparent and integral opportunities.

God will not choose for us, because choice is our responsibility.

We all have a little voice inside of us that whispers—and sometimes shouts—to warn us and guide us. We know when we're before some sort of charlatan. We know when there's a snake oil salesman before us. We know when there is a relationship that's not transparent, and someone is hiding something. We know this. By instinct, whatever it may be. Women might say it's their female intuition. Men might call it a gut feeling. Whatever it is, it's there.

We all have that natural instinct that drives us toward purity. We're driven by something that's raw, that's untouched, that's virgin, that's holy, that's righteous. That's the direction that little voice guides us toward.

And that's what drove Mary Magdalene that day. The fact is that she could have continued to sit and stay in her circumstance, but she didn't. She chose to run toward something that was even greater. That was her impetus: She chose.

It all begins with the choice. The idea that God is going to come down from heaven and make the choice for you is preposterous. That's not the way the Lord works. We make the choice, and when we do, we activate the divine. Choice activates the divine. Choice activates God's purpose. And God will not choose for us, because choice is our responsibility.

In every single day, every single morning that we wake up, we have choices to make. Will that day be your greatest day? Will it be a mediocre day? Will you overcome the circumstances, the calls, the challenges that may come that day?

It can be little things, or it can be big things, but as you make your choices you want to make sure they're all aiming to do the right thing. Don't pick what's expedient. Don't pick what's easy. Don't pick what's most convenient, or fastest. Pick what's right.

And here is the beautiful, the free—and freeing—part: It's totally up to you.

> *Choice activates the divine. Choice activates God's purpose.*

You also shouldn't wait until the choice is upon you to make your decision. Don't wait until you reach the fork in the road to determine which way you want to go. It's not to choose once the circumstance arises, it's to choose beforehand.

Looking at it that way, I don't see problems or challenges; I see opportunities, because the challenge really is an opportunity.

I see problems as the prophetic foreshadowing of the promise. I see every mistake as the precedent to a miracle. So the moment that the mistake, the problem, or the challenge comes, I see an opportunity—and I have already made my choice. I already know what direction I'm going. I'm just acting on the choice I made.

I don't wait to say, "Well, I have this call. What do I do now? Let me choose." I wake up in the morning and say:

"I've decided. I'm determined. My choice is made. Regardless of what comes my way, here's what I've chosen. I've chosen to do good and not wrong. I've chosen to lift and not bring down. I've chosen to be faithful to my Spiritual DNA, and not to acquiesce to circumstances. I've chosen to look beyond the storm and to see what God has for me on this day.

"I know that God has something for me on this day. This day. Not tomorrow, but this day. I need to find it and I have chosen this morning to discover it. Regardless of the costs, I will discover it."

That's the choice we should make.

Chapter 14

RUN TO YOUR FIRST PLACE

M ary Magdalene was going someplace. She wasn't just running in circles and wailing and crying because she lost the person who was so important in her life. She obviously wasn't just sitting. But sometimes, in our own lives, we do. We just sit and wait. Or we run in circles. Not literally, although maybe sometimes we do that, too. But we run in circles figuratively: we do the same thing over and over and over again. And often it is the wrong thing.

That's not the way to do it. If it's not working, we have to run someplace.

But it can't be just anyplace. We have to run someplace, and it has to be our First Place.

What do I mean by that?

Many of us live in a secular, Second Place world. We're not living our First Place objective or our First Place purpose.

Here's an example from Scripture, within the book of Genesis:[1]

The Bible tells us that Abraham had an Ishmael before he had an Isaac.

Abraham wanted a son. And, of course, he jumped the gun. Abraham entered into a relationship with a concubine named Hagar. Instead of waiting upon God, who had promised Abraham and his wife things, they jumped the gun.

That speaks to our human nature, because we sometimes just can't wait upon the Lord. It's so difficult to say, be still. That's because we live in an instantaneous gratification world. And the most difficult thing we can do is what the Bible tells us we should do: be still and know that God is God. It's hard to be still and let God do his work. We want it now.

---

1   Genesis 16–21.

Abraham and Hagar were no different. They jumped the gun, and Abraham had his relationship with Hagar and they had Ishmael. Now, Abraham really believed that Ishmael was the fulfillment of his promise, that Ishmael was the answer to his prayer. So he walked around with Ishmael saying, "I prayed, and regardless of how I got him, I got him. I have the heir to the family name, the heir to the heritage, the heir to the rams and to the livestock. I've got my son. I have my First Place."

What he did not understand is that later on, there would be Isaac. So, while Abraham walked around with Ishmael, he really thought that he had his First Place. But then Isaac came along, as promised by God, the one who God said He would make His covenant with, and Abraham realized, "Wait a minute. I've been walking around with Second Place, up until now."

There are many people in the world today, many of us, who may be in a Second Place job, in that Second Place setting, in that Second Place mindset, in a Second Place relationship with God. Whatever that Second Place thing may be, we are wandering around satisfied with it, not realizing that God has a First Place for us.

Second Place feels *good enough*, so we never go for great. We pull into the first fast-food joint we see instead of holding off to find a place with good, healthy food. We get up and go to work every day at a job that's *good enough*— it pays the bills, and it's not too bad, but it's never really satisfying. Second Place will deaden the hunger and keep you content, but it will never fill you or make you truly happy.

Just ask my friend Gilberto Velez. He had a successful career as a doctor, rising over the years until he was the director of clinical services for the Laredo State Mental Health Mental Retardation Center. He supervised physicians, nurses, pharmacists, psychologists, and their departments, as well as headed up the Crisis Intervention Unit and Medical Records.

That's pretty prestigious stuff—a doctor, making good money, and in charge of a sizeable staff with a truly important function. He was helping make sick people get better! What could be more important—or more satisfying—than that?

But it wasn't. He was helping lives, but he wanted to change them. In 1997, he quit and founded a church near that state facility where he had worked. He had to take a serious pay cut, but the rewards, he felt, would be worth it.

It was. Now he's the head of a successful megachurch, tending to the spiritual health of a flock of more than two thousand.

His Second Place had been good and rewarding, but God did not make us for Ishmael. God made us for Isaac.

The message is this: We need to discover who our Isaac is. We need to discover what our First Place objective may be so that we are not just running randomly. So that we are not running sporadically. So that we are not running without any direction. We need to identify our true First Place goal so that we know where we are going.

> *We need to discover our First Place objective so that we know where we are going.*

There are those out there who want to teach that the enemy—Satan, the devil, the opposite force, whatever you call it—would love to make sure you never have anything.

I disagree with that.

I think the devil would love to see us have something, but not what we should have.

Let me explain why.

The moment we have nothing, we will search for it. This whole idea that the enemy would like to take everything away and leave us with nothing is absurd. Because the moment we have nothing we'll search for it. And in searching we may actually find the truth.

If someone wants to keep us from discovering the truth, a much better strategy is to give us something that will satisfy us: Let me give you that Milky Way bar that will give you the illusion that you're actually full when you're not really full.

That's what we continuously receive. We continuously get the Milky Way bars in life. We get the continual short-term satisfaction that will distract us from our long-term fulfillment. We settle for second and third, for silver and bronze instead of gold.

Often enough, we do it to ourselves. It's easier. Abraham didn't want to wait. It was easier and more convenient to go to Hagar—and he could have what he wanted now. He was impatient. He wasn't willing to hold on and wait for God's promise to come true. He had the promise. God told him his First Place was coming. But Abraham wanted it *now*.

Does that ever happen to you? Do you go into the kitchen looking for something to eat, and settle for the first thing you see? Or the easiest? Sometimes do you tell yourself you're going to make yourself a nice healthy sandwich, or heat up some soup, and end up grabbing the bag of potato chips off the shelf?

That's Second Place. And, unfortunately, we don't just do it in the little things in life like potato chips. We do it with the big things, too. We don't go back to night school to get that training that will allow us to get a better job, or to move up at the one we're at. We just keep punching the clock. Hey, it pays the bills, right?

We settle for Ishmael instead of waiting for Isaac.

Mary Magdalene didn't. She went to her First Place. She knew where she was going.

How do I know I'm running in the right direction? How do I know I'm running on the right course? How do I know I'm walking with my Isaac instead of my Ishmael? How do I know?

You know by the circumstances you're in. And you know you're going in the right direction when you are experiencing confrontation, when obstacles come your way. I know this sounds contradictory, but it's true: obstacles would not come your way if you were not going in the right direction.

> *Obstacles do one of two things: They push you in the right direction, or they catapult you to a higher place.*

There are things in our lives that would love to stop us from really reaching our full potential, from accomplishing that purpose, from living exceedingly, abundantly, and above all.

Some come from the outside; some are of our own making.

There are tragedies that are truly beyond our control—that drunk driver, that tragic accident, that sickness. At the end of the day, they don't speak to where I come from, they speak to where I'm going to. They don't speak for what I've done wrong; they speak to what I've done right.

That's not to say that everything in our lives is the result of external forces. I would argue that many of the things that happen in our lives—not everything, not even half, but many things—happen as a result of our own doing. We make bad choices. We follow the path of temptation instead of the path of righteousness. We give up when we should stand up.

Confrontation, tragedies, and problems, along with the impediments and obstructions we create for ourselves—they are all obstacles. And they all will do one of two things: They will push you in the right direction, or they will catapult you to a higher place.

In other words, obstacles will expose where you should go, or they will align you in your prophetic alignment with where you need to go. They will reveal, or they will direct. If you're totally lost, your obstacles will illuminate the goal. If you're struggling, they will help you get in line, to see the path *and* what you need to do to get there.

The very fact that you're running into obstacles means you're going the right way.

I know I'm going the right way when I'm running in darkness, and I have very few companions with me, but in my heart there is peace. I know I'm going the right way when I see things that others don't see. I know I'm going the right way when I'm running to help others, not selfishly, not for me. And I know I'm going the right way when I see obstacles. But I don't let them stop me—I use them to guide me along my way, to show me my purpose, or to propel me to new heights.

PRINCIPLE TWO

FAITH AND FEAR ALWAYS RUN TOGETHER

Chapter 15

PROBLEMS AND PROMISES

Faith and fear always run together. It's an inevitable partnership. It exists in every single level of reality, be it spiritual, physical, metaphysical, or cosmic. You can measure what exists by looking for its equivalent counterpart—in nature, in physics and mathematics, in relationships and proportionality. Even in Newtonian principles: the equal and opposite reaction to every action. In everything we see, in everything embedded within our reality, what we deal with are dualities.

For that very reason, we're never confronted with just "problems." A problem is always accompanied by a promise. There are always two sides to absolutely everything that we participate in, that we are challenged by in life. And faith and fear are the most significant.

I don't find it to be a mere coincidence that it was Peter and John running together on that day, on the third day. Each personified, each embodied, our own personal dichotomous existence. Each and every one of us, we walk with faith and fear. In some sort of utopian, Pollyannaish presentation, it's just faith. In the hyperbole of spiritualism it's just faith. But reality dictates that wherever faith exists there will also be fear.

> ***A problem is always accompanied by a promise.***

Whenever we have a dream, we will probably have to face a couple of nightmares that rise up to quash the dream. Whenever we have an opportunity we're going to have to face some hurdles and obstacles.

It's that Newtonian principle again, as applied toward our daily journey. It's a continuation of nature, a continuation of God's creation—there was daylight and there was nighttime. Force and counterforce. We similarly experience the same.

I see it from a positive light. The way I see it, for every problem there must be a simultaneous promise. For every valley there must be a mountain. For every mistake there must be a miracle. For every single difficult circumstance there must be an equal positive circumstance.

So, when I feel fear I should feel hope. When I feel fear I should find my faith.

And when we have faith, we will be able to recognize our fear for what it is. We know that fear is out there. You know that when you lay your little baby down to sleep, you worry that she'll be fine through the night. You know when you read about horrible economic news, you fear that you could be laid off at work. You know when you go to launch your own business, you worry that it might fail. But when you have faith, you can face your fear and know that it is not there to hurt you, it's there to warn you, to make you consider all the things you can do to make sure things don't go wrong, and to remind you to prepare yourself in case something does.

Fear exists. But so does faith. It's right there, with the fear. It's right next to it. Actually, at times it can be embedded in it. And all we have to do is remove the layer of grave clothes shrouding it. All we have to do is look past the fear to find the faith, because fear's presence guarantees faith's promise. It is that very presence of fear, it is the existence of fear, that assures us that faith has a promise.

It is possible to run in faith, next to fear. It is possible to pursue our dream, and to pursue the goal, to pursue the Wow! Factor, the blessing, the "It," the fulfillment, that quintessential moment at the apex of satisfaction, intrinsically and extrinsically.

Can we fulfill our dream? Can we reach our exceedingly, abundantly, above all? We can. Even with fear at our side.

Now, it's important to look at the semantics here. Never have I stated that this is *with* fear, or *in* fear. We're running with fear at our side.

> *Fear's presence guarantees faith's promise.*

To explain, let's go back to the laws of nature, back to the different levels of reality. It is that equal and opposite reaction. It's embedded throughout nature, throughout creation, throughout our journeys—for every Goliath there must be a David, and for every Pharaoh there must be a Moses.

We see it even illustrated in the circle of life: for every person that passes away on this planet, there is another born simultaneously. It's embedded in every single component of our life.

Fear and faith exist in the same way. We need to understand that we are never going to be able to separate ourselves completely from the notion or the idea or the existence of fear. Fear's presence tells me that faith must be nearby with a promise in its hand waiting for me to take it. The very fact that we are confronting that fear means that its opposite, faith, is with me.

So, on our journey through life, on our way on the path of miracles, we shouldn't fear fear. We shouldn't cower and cringe. When we find fear, we should find strength. And we need to know—know!—that the presence of that fear means that faith is with us.

Chapter 16

FAITH ARRIVES FIRST

Peter and John ran together, but John—faith—got there first.[1]

Now, in John arriving there first, it speaks volumes.

It tells us that faith and fear may run together, your nightmare may mock you as you have your dream, but your dream will always get there first. Faith will always get there first.

It teaches us that at the end of the day you may have to run with weakness, you may have to run with that shortcoming, you may not be perfect. There may be areas in your life that you struggle with. But if you walk *in* faith and walk *with* faith and walk *through* faith and walk *by* faith to believe, then there is a guarantee, a biblical and divine principle, a God-given principle, which is: If you do it by faith, faith will always get there first.

You may have to survive while looking and seeing fear at your side every day, while having to see that nightmare. But if you stay focused and run straight ahead you'll reach there first. Faith will always get there first.

> *If you do it by faith, faith will always get there first.*

But the amazing thing is this: John did not go in first. All he did was glance. If you can picture this: John arrives there first, but he just glances in and says, "I knew it!" In essence, it was, "Yes!"

All faith needs to do is look. Faith is satisfied with the hearing and the seeing.

It was fear—Peter the denier; Peter, the roosters crow thrice—that drove

---

1   John 20:4.

Peter, who needed to go beyond the glance and needed to step in. Because fear will never be changed into faith without transformation and experience.

Faith is believing in what is not seen; it is the conviction of things hoped for.[2]

But fear needs to go inside and look around and touch the spot and make sure the body is gone and that the only thing left is the folded linens, the grave clothes left behind. Fear needs to step into the corridor and know for sure that there's no one there. Fear needs evidence to become faith. Fear needs proof. Fear needs to be injected with the experiential, the affective—emotionally, spiritually, and physically. It needs to be completely overwhelmed by the reality.

And in Peter's case it was the most overwhelming reality of all—Jesus wasn't there.

> *Fear will never be changed into faith without transformation and experience.*

The fact that Peter stepped in and had his moment while John stayed on the outskirts, and then he accompanied him on the run back, is just amazing to me. What I think is just so marvelous is that even though faith got there first, it didn't go in. Instead of rushing in itself, faith opened up the way and pushed fear in. Basically, in a nutshell, faith said, "Look! I told you so."

John arrives first and pushes Peter forward, so Peter can confront his fear.

Fear and faith always run together, but faith arrives first to push fear forward to find the evidence it needs. Faith arrives first to help us overcome our fears. Faith arrives first to give us the push we need, at the moment that we most need it.

---

2   Hebrews 11:1.

Chapter 17

OVERCOMING OUR FEAR

There are some of us in our journeys who sometimes need more than just a glance. We're like Peter. We need a lot more than just seeing it. We need to experience it.

That's fine. That's how we overcome our fear.

My fear will convert into faith the moment I'm willing to step in. This is part of Peter's legacy. He's the one who always stepped in. He stepped into the water when everyone else stayed on the boat.[1] He stepped into the empty tomb and discovered the folded linens.[2]

Is it this Peter the fearful who stepped on water? Absolutely not. Was it Peter the fearful who cut the ear of the soldier off when he went to arrest Jesus? Absolutely not. Was it Peter the fearful who stepped into the empty tomb, alone? Absolutely not.

So how do we overcome the fear in our own lives? The same way. By stepping in. Think about it: Is there anything scarier than entering a tomb? Who among us has entered a mausoleum at night? It is terrifying! It's the stuff horror movies are made of!

When we are challenged by that moment, by that circumstance, we have two choices. We have a choice of running away from the tomb or running toward it. What the story of Peter and John running tells us is that we can run even when our name is fear, not faith. We can run as Peter or John, every single day.

> *My fear will transform to faith the moment I dare to step in*
> *and confront that circumstance.*

---

1   Matthew 14:29.
2   John 20:5–6.

There will be days we wake up as Peter, and there will be days we wake up more like John. And in my Peter days, in my Peter moments, it is the audacity to step in that will carry me forward, that will take me toward my goal. It's the courage and the wherewithal to confront my fear by stepping in that will propel me onward on the path of miracles.

What is it that catapults me to step in? How is it that I am able to step past my fear, overcome my trepidation, rise above my apprehension and go into that place? By understanding the principle that there is an assurance, a truth, a biblical and divine and cosmic reality that if I do step in, my fear will change and transform into faith; that I will see what I need and experience it.

There will be transformation the moment I dare to step in and confront that circumstance.

So, in my darkest moments, in the times when I am doubting myself, I have to step forward and believe that I can make it. I have to believe that God has those treasures for me. I have to believe that God already has made a way for me.

But there's a prerequisite to receiving those treasures and of finding the way God has prepared: I need to confront my deepest fear at my darkest hour in the most solitary of places—in your dark night of the soul.

> *There is life after your most difficult moment.*

The secret of great success, the difference between good and great, the difference between mediocrity and exceedingly, abundantly, above all is running at your darkest hour and confronting your greatest fear, in the most solitary circumstances.

That's what's going to make the difference.

The difference between having a mediocre business or a mediocre dream or a mediocre moment and having great ones, the difference between so-so and the Wow! Factor—that apex, that epitome of fulfillment and satisfaction, of reaching the Now Moments where God's perfect will for your life, where God's perfect destiny is completely unfolded—is stepping in and confronting your greatest fear.

It's the difference between a C and an A+. And, tell me, when you're looking back at it all, reviewing where you've been and what you've had and what you've done in your life, do you really want it to be a C? Do you really want it to be so-so? Do you really want to look back at your life and say it was *good enough*?

No. That's not what living is about. It's not about living 70 percent. It's not about living 50 percent. It's not about living 80 percent or 90 percent.

What if we could live 100 percent in God's perfect, divine destiny? At 100 percent in God's purpose for our lives? What if everything that God has for us—the exceedingly, abundantly, above all—can actually be lived out and realized right now? Not as the end of the journey, not when I'm eighty-three years old, right before the epitaph, not at that moment, but what if we could live 100 percent in the fullness of what God has for us every single day of our lives?

What if the kingdom of God could become a reality in my life every single day? What if heaven can touch Earth through my life every single day?

It can. That's what the Bible says: "For behold, the kingdom of God is in your midst."[3] It can do that when I'm willing to step into that dark place at the darkest hour, when my name is fear. It's easy when my name is faith. It's easy when I believe it and see it, and I'm so overwhelmed by security and all the circumstances are wonderful.

But it's not so easy when I've just finished denying him, when I just, in essence, turned my back on my destiny and turned my back on my purpose. It's not so easy right after your fall and your failure. Right after you were turned down for that business opportunity. Right after your investments failed miserably. Right after you receive your rejection notice. Right after your divorce. Right after that moment of failure and weakness. Right after.

But—and this is the audacity of this presentation—right after you deny, right after you've been burned, right after, you *can* get up and step into the place that you thought you should not step into.

> *The kingdom of God can become a reality in your life, and heaven can touch Earth through your life, every single day.*

---

3 Luke 17:21.

Let's look beyond the religious and faith perspective of the resurrected Christ. Let's look at the natural picture if we can, at that moment that speaks of life right after our crucifixion, life after our most difficult circumstance. Life after we are abandoned and we are nailed and we bleed and we have a crown of thorns, which means from our head to our cerebral cortex to our minds and our thoughts and every part of our body; when we are pierced, when we are wounded and we are left for dead, and everything inside of us spilt out—life after that.

That's the message of the third day: that there is life after your most difficult moment. There is life after your crucifixion. There is life after your Golgotha experience. There is life after you're wounded. There is life after you're stripped of your clothes. There is life after you're given cheap wine to drink. There is life after that.

Can you reclaim your destiny immediately after that? Yes.

Chapter 18

USING FEAR TO HELP US

If there is anyone who should not have been in that tomb on that third day, if there is anyone who should not have run, if there was anyone who should not have accompanied John, if there was anyone who was disqualified, it was Peter.

There was one other who should not have been there, and he wasn't. He couldn't be. The other one who should not have been there died. He was disqualified. He *quit*! He gave up on God's infinite love and mercy. That other one who should not have been there and wasn't, of course, was Judas.

But, believe me, if there's anyone among those who remained who should not have been there, who was so afraid of that whole experience, at that quintessential historic moment, at that moment of life abundant, at that moment that speaks to us, it was Peter.

No one should have been more disqualified than Mr. Fear. But he stepped in. And he stepped in because he was accustomed to stepping in. There's something about fear that at times acts as a great impetus and motivator.

Faith is the assurance and the conviction of things hoped for and not seen. Faith doesn't need to take any risks. Faith believes.

Fear does not believe. Fear takes risks.

> *At times we can use our fear in order to prove our fear wrong.*

Peter, Mr. Fear, was willing to take risks on more than one occasion. Now, if he was fearful, why would he dare to take risks? Because fear takes risks. At times we use our fear in order to prove our fear wrong. Fear acts as an adrenaline booster. It acts as an intrinsic motivation, even if only for a moment. It only takes one momentary glimpse.

Faith believes all the time. But fear hides in the shadows. We know that from Peter denying Christ and what he did afterward. Fear is uncomfortable with opportunities, dreads confrontation. But fear also has this intrinsic inclination to take risks. So it steps in. The discovery took place in a spot where it never, never, ever, ever should have stepped into.

But fear takes risks. It stepped in. Because fear is more afraid of not knowing. The greatest fear that fear has is not knowing whether or not it can step into a place where it will be forever transformed. Fear can handle so many other things. Fear can face the fear of failure, the fear of rejection. But the fear of not knowing? Can fear live with not knowing? The answer is *no*.

What we fear, and the magnitude of our fear, is equivalent to the magnitude of our faith. My fear is proportional to my faith. If I fear falling thirty steps it means my faith is really projecting me to be launched thirty steps above.

So that fear factor works for me, not against me, as long as I walk and run next to it and not in it. As long as I walk and run next to it and not in it, fear will never capture me. It can't capture me, but I can capture it. I can capture that fear, and I can use that energy to catapult me. That fear—fear of failure; fear of rejection; fear of disappointment; fear of loneliness; fear of never reaching the goal; fear of never living exceedingly, abundantly, above all; fear of losing my family; fear of losing my sanity; fear of whatever it may be; of fear itself; the fear of not doing the right thing—that fear will act as a catalyst for faith to arrive in our journey.

> *Fear works for me, not against me, as long as I walk and run next to it and not in it.*

Faith and fear will always run together. Your dream will always be accompanied by a nightmare. But I would like to change the narrative, turn it around, and say:

Your nightmare will always be accompanied by a dream.

Instead of saying your success will always be accompanied by failure, I would rather say that wherever you see failure, your success cannot be too far away. Wherever you see brokenness, wholeness cannot be too far away. Because they always run together. The equal and opposite always run together. Failure may walk right next to you, but faith is in you. So success cannot be too far away.

Chapter 19

FINDING OURSELVES IN SOLITUDE

Peter represents fear. But Peter also represents impetuousness, angst, and every person who has ever tried and stumbled. Fear causes doubt. It undermines our confidence and makes us anxious. And, as Peter showed us as he walked across the water, fear causes us to falter and fall.

John represents faith, but he also represents loneliness and solitude. He's lost his mentor, he's lost his guide, and, so, he is alone.

Of course, John being faith, even though he is alone and he is on his own to a degree, he is still comforted by the reality of his faith, by his sheer belief that at the end of the day he will be back with his master. He has the unbridled conviction that he understands the end already. He says, "I understand the last chapter before the first one was read or written."

He understood that. So he doesn't need to step into a moment of solitude to confront himself, because faith counters multitudes of loneliness and multitudes of sins and multitudes of solitude.

> *In solitude we find ourselves.*

Peter, though, being in fear, needed to step into solitude. There is a difference between stepping into it, where you're surrounded by it, and carrying it. John carried it, but I wholeheartedly believe that he left it right there at the edge of the tomb. Just by seeing. By glimpsing. By realizing, "Aha! I knew it. I knew it all the time. He promised it. I believe it. I'm here to affirm it. I knew it."

John may have been alone all of a sudden without Jesus, but he was not lonely—because he knew what awaited him. Peter is lonely, even when he's with Jesus. We see the evidence of that by some of the moments of Peter's confrontation.

> *Once we find ourselves, and are at peace with ourselves,*
> *we are never lonely.*

That's why Peter needed to step into solitude, to be truly alone, to recognize that he could do it on his own, that he could stand on his own, that he could face his fear all on his own, all alone, and that he was not lonely. In solitude, he could find himself. And once we find ourselves, and are at peace with ourselves, we are never lonely.

So we need to be alone, to be able to figure out that we're not lonely. We need to have the time to ourselves to see that we have these things in our lives, and that we have a purpose and there are those rewards for us.

In solitude we find ourselves, the same way that Peter did.

Chapter 20

FEAR AND FAITH NEED
EACH OTHER

You really can't have faith without walking next to fear. You really can't experience the fullness of the faith component without having some kind of fear confrontation. They need each other.

This entire idea, this oversold concept, where everything is absolutely positive and if you know it and claim it, it's yours and life is just a bed of roses—it's wrong! I mean, the fact is, we're selling people just a crock of soft goods out there.

The fact of the matter is that there will be times when we will walk with fear, when we are confronted with very difficult circumstances. But fear and faith need each other. I would say that fear can't succeed without faith and faith can't succeed without fear.

As comfortable as you may be in life, fear will push you to go forward, because you're not satisfied with that, because you fear that you're missing out on something else ahead of you. You fear that this may be taken away from you.

I compare it to immigrant stories and Shoah survivor stories, to the stories of those people who say, "We lost it all. We came here to go forward." They survived; then they succeeded.

> *Fear can't succeed without faith and faith can't succeed without fear.*

Faith got them through the horrors they had to suffer through, but it was fear that pushed them on. They had lost it all once, and barely came out with their lives. But having been through that, they knew it could happen again. They knew—and they feared—that it could all be taken away again. So they tried even harder. So many of them rebuilt what they had had, and then some.

Let's take a look at those survivors. Let's take a look at survivors of the Jewish Shoah. Let's look at survivors of the Rwandan genocide. Let's look at the most recent refugees from the Khmer Rouge in Cambodia. Let's look at the pogroms in the last one hundred years, including the Armenians with the Turks at the beginning of the twentieth century.

If you read the personal narratives and stories of the people who come out of these ethnic cleansings, as they have been euphemized, you see that their response is that they run. They run through the darkness and they step into circumstances where others would not step in, even with fear. And they're very protective of what they have because of their fear of repeating history, of losing it all—their property, their belongings, even their lives.

It's fear and faith again. They have the faith that was sufficient to recover after the most difficult and horrible circumstances, absolutely horrendous circumstances. However, even though those times are behind them, fear never completely went away. They had the faith to recover. But they see that having that bit of fear, without completely acquiescing to it—that one little fear gene, one little DNA thread—serves to remind them that this could happen again, unless they're cautious.

> *Fear runs from the past, but faith runs toward the future.*

But the fear doesn't work alone. The fear keeps us looking back over our shoulder to see if the past is coming again to repeat itself. But faith looks ahead, toward what can be. Fear runs from the past, but faith runs toward the future.

Peter ran from the past. But John ran toward the future. Peter was running away from his denial. He was running away from his failure. He was running from the past. Fear runs from the past. From the past missed opportunities. From the past hurts. From the past pain. From the past circumstances.

Fear runs from the past. Fear runs from fear. Fear runs from rejection.

Faith runs toward healing. It runs toward restoration. It's not a matter of semantic nitpicking. It's really important to understand the context—one ran from; the other ran toward.

Peter was running away from the cross. He was running away from betrayal. He was running away from denial. He was running away from the wounds and the bruises of forgiveness. But he ran.

We have to be careful, though. I don't want to reinforce the notion that if you are rejected and you go through difficult situations and have difficult relationships that you should run away from new opportunities. You shouldn't. You need to let that energy, the energy from the fear, catapult you toward a place of confrontation.

For John, the tomb was a place of affirmation.

For Peter it was a place of confrontation.

Peter ran away from his past, but in essence ran toward a moment of confrontation where he had no other choice but to come face-to-face with what was both his greatest anxiety and his greatest reward.

Think about it. If he walks in there, and Christ's body is still in there, then Peter's denial becomes less impactful. But if he walks in there, and there's evidence of a viable resurrection—not that the body was stolen, but a viable resurrection—then he has proof.

> *We must run when we are fearful in order to confront*
> *the very things that we fear.*

So, yes, one runs away from the past and the other one runs toward the future, but your running fear will always run toward a moment of confrontation. We must run when we are fearful in order to confront the very things that we fear. Let's have a head-on heart-to-heart.

In other words, I would tell someone who has come out of a bad relationship, or a series of bad relationships, you can't run away from all relationships. You can't run away in a panic the instant someone shows an interest, or when you think you're starting to care. I would tell that woman who is running away from that relationship—that woman who went through a tumultuous relationship, a tumultuous divorce; that woman who was abused physically, emotionally, mentally, intellectually, sexually, spiritually, who sacrificed her career for that marriage that became nothing through the infidelity of a prior husband—I would tell her: Eventually you will end up at the empty tomb.

She may have met other men since that relationship ended. Great men may have come to her, who really fit the bill, but she ran away from them.

You can't run foolishly into every relationship that presents itself, of course. That's just running. But you can't run away from every one that presents itself, either. You have to be wise, but you have to be willing to confront your fear. Eventually you will end up at the empty tomb.

The sooner you realize that, the sooner you can get on with your life and find out that chapter two is actually greater than chapter one.

That's what happened to my blessed friend Aurea Luz. Abandoned by her first husband, Aurea dedicated herself to raising her two small children, and keeping them safe from the drug dealers and criminals in the neighborhoods surrounding her tiny apartment in New York. She worked hard to provide for them, taking two or three buses to get to the factory where she earned minimum wage sewing. She didn't have time for new love. And she didn't want it. Her experience had made her determined never to marry again.

And she never took a government handout. She continued to believe that if she worked hard and persevered, God would reward her with exceedingly, abundantly, above all, and that her pain would convert into prosperity.

After fifteen years alone, Aurea's faith was rewarded, in ways beyond anything she ever expected. A man she had seen when she was younger, but had never spoken to, came back into her life.

Eusebio had become single, and was tired of being alone. He started praying for a soul mate. His son knew Aurea, and gave Eusebio her phone number. After a year of phone conversations, they decided to meet personally. This time, it was love at first sight. They got married a day later.

But God wasn't finished granting Aurea and Eusebio miracles.

The company he worked at kept giving him raises, and he started to invest in real estate. As the Bible says, "remember the Lord your God, for it is He who gives you the ability to produce wealth."[1]

Now they both are retired and living in a dream chateau in the Caribbean. They own multiple properties and continue to serve God, reminding her grandchildren that, "according to your faith will it be done to you."[2]

---

1 Deuteronomy 8:18.
2 Matthew 9:29.

Chapter 21

CONFRONT YOUR FEAR

The truth is that you're born to run until eventually you have to confront your greatest fear. It's either going to occur today, in twenty, thirty, or forty years, or on your deathbed. But it is inevitable. You will not die without confronting that great fear. Even if it's on your deathbed.

And I would rather it happen for you today. Confront it and be transformed. That's deliverance.

Every single day that you don't confront your fear is a missed opportunity to have your moment. It is a missed opportunity to live life to the fullest. It is a day that you did not live. You lived in your physical existence, yes. You lived superficially. But that's not living. Existence, yes; living, no.

There's a difference between existing and living. You existed that day, but you did not live. You occupied space. You occupied the reality between matter and antimatter. Your energy being on this planet remains kinetic, it remains as potential; but it's not applied energy, you just exist. You take up space.

> *Confront your fear and be transformed. That's deliverance.*

But living, *living!*—that's waking up every day ready to go and having a purpose for your life. Waking up every single day with destiny. Waking up every single day with that Kingdom Culture, with that God-given DNA, knowing that you will work hard to make sure that what you leave behind is better than what you've taken. And that your children and your children's children will continue this and you're going to enrich their lives as they enrich your life.

It's living every single day knowing that you're doing God's perfect will. Knowing that your vertical connections—to heaven and God—have horizontal consequences right here on Earth. Knowing that you are going to meet people that day whom you will change and impact. Knowing that you have opportunities on that day to change lives. Knowing that people will arrive on that day, and it is not coincidence—not if we believe in God, not if we believe in destiny.

But we also marry that with free will and choices. Then, at the macro level, we do understand that these are not some serendipitous occurrences, but rather that God gives us opportunities to impact and change and transform. And every life that I change enriches my life. I enrich theirs, which enriches mine, and we enrich our humanity and our brotherhood collectively.

> *Confront your fear and be transformed; avoid it and be enslaved.*

Every single day that I do not confront, every day that I continue to avoid, I avoid a day of living and I embrace a day of just mere existence.

And I don't want to spend my life living to die; I'm dying to live. I am willing to crucify myself daily in order to live. I'm dying to live. I don't live to die.

I wake up every morning dying to live. I get up and go out and I make sure that I crucify my fear, my trepidation, my anxiety, my insecurity, my weaknesses, my vice, my Flesh Man—that thing that does not permit me to fully live. That decision, that wrong decision, that erroneous inclination. The roar of the animal kingdom in me. The part that doesn't reason things out in logic and rationale, but rather that I react to. I react to my carnal desires. I react even, to a degree, to my emotional desires. That is what I must crucify daily. If not, I'm just existing.

So every single day I am dying to live. Every single day.

I look at my fear, and I say, "You're dead." That's the thought that comes to my mind. I address it immediately. I confront it, not avoid it. And I will say, "You have no authority over me—GET BEHIND ME, SATAN!"[1]

---

1   Matthew 16:23.

The good news is that every single day I have the ability, the wherewithal, the God-given DNA, to put that fear away.

On the other side of the coin—I wouldn't say it's bad news, but it's reality—every single morning fear is there again. It is *not* a once-and-for-all removal and elimination of the fear component. It is a *daily* confrontation with fear. "We must LEARN not to be afraid!" as Pope John Paul II reminded all Christians.

> *Every single day that you don't confront your fear is a missed opportunity to live life to the fullest.*

We all have fear. I, too, fear all the things I mentioned above. I have the fear of losing it all; the fear of making decisions that will impact hundreds of thousands and millions that will be the wrong decision; fear of making the wrong choices; fear of, in my inclination toward speaking for those who can't speak for themselves, doing more harm than good; fear of pride; fear of arrogance; fear of believing that I can do this by myself; fear of being dependent on my own energy and strength exclusively.

But I don't let my fears capture me. I confront them. And I master them.

The fears that I can be unfaithful to my wife or I can be unfaithful to my children and my legacy and my heritage—I confront them. The fears that make me doubt and hesitate and waver—I confront them.

They will come. They're there. Confront them.

Every single day.

Chapter 22

HIDING FROM OUR FEAR

I t's no secret that people hide from their fear through drugs. They hide through alcohol, and they hide through sex, through carnal pleasures. They're not seeking pleasure; they're seeking escape. They may *say* they want to be cured of their fear, but they're lying. A cure is painful. All they want is relief.

But that doesn't work. That's not curing our fear, or facing our fear. That's hiding from fear, finding some momentary escape from fear that only worsens it.

We use these escapes to avoid the daylight, for the daylight can shine a light on our shortcomings, on our fear. Because we're walking with fear, our notion is to hide in the shadows and to hide under something—drugs, sex, relationships, gambling, addictions, compulsive behavior. These actions speak more to our fears than anything else.

In our effort to hide from our fears, we harm ourselves. Instead of facing the pain, we cause more pain—for ourselves and those around us, for those we love. Instead of dealing with the real problem, we add to our problems. It never gets better when we hide from our fear. It only gets worse.

> *Fear + Confrontation = Revelation of faith.*

That is why I stress the urgency of confrontation that will lead to revelation, the urgency of confronting that fear in order to reveal the faith. It's a simple little formula that counters the fear, and lets our faith shine: Fear + Confrontation = Revelation of faith.

What we have today, in our twenty-first-century setting, is moments of intervention. These individuals who struggle with addiction at times experience an intervention from family members and loved ones. They find themselves surrounded by people who care. Intervention is de facto confrontation.

But it's not us doing the confronting. That's others doing it for us. Until we can confront our fears ourselves, it's not enough. That's why people backslide.

We do need running partners. That running partner actually becomes our firewall. But they can't do it for me.

I have to confront my fears myself if I am really going to change my life.

There is a lot of research out there that substantiates that there is greater success when an individual confronts his addiction, where it is self-motivated. God bless all the interventions; however, many of the addicts who go through interventions become repeat offenders! After the intervention, after staying sober six or eight months, one year, many of those who experience the intervention—where it's not self-motivated, where there is not the confrontation but rather this gathering of "let's get some help for you"—they repeat.

But those who confront it for themselves, those who say, "I need to turn my life around," have a greater success rate. They have a much greater chance of changing permanently, of kicking their habit and cleaning up their life, when they want to change for themselves, when there is self-confrontation. Even when people are forced to get treatment, the success comes when they accept the fact that they need to change. Other people saying it doesn't make it happen. People have to recognize it for themselves.

> *I have to confront my fears myself if I am really going to change my life.*

True success will occur when there is self-confrontation. When you confront fear. Others can't do it for you. Others can't carry you to the tomb. Others can't hold your eyes open and make you see. It's wonderful to see John stay right there, just glimpse and stay on the edge. John doesn't go through at all. Nothing in Scripture at all says that John went into the tomb to see for himself. Peter went in.

He had to. Peter had to go in for himself. He had to see for himself. Peter, Mr. Fear, had to go in and face his fears—for himself! That experience, that stepping in, that confrontation changed him. He did it. And he changed. He faced his fear, and he transformed.

Someone once said that true courage is not the lack of fear; true courage is doing what you have to do even when you're afraid.

That means: You have to face your fear. You have to confront it. You have to step in, in spite of it.

If John had gone in and seen the tomb was empty and come out and told Peter, it wouldn't have been the same. If John had pulled Peter in—and he had somehow been able to force Peter to look and see—it wouldn't have been the same. If he had gone in halfheartedly or against his will, Peter could have still made excuses. He could have still denied. If he didn't do it for himself, and face his fear for himself, the chance is—no, the probability is— he would not have changed. Or he would have only changed temporarily.

That's what happens in the interventions we do *for* people instead of *with* them.

At the same time, we don't want to say don't intervene at all, because sometimes people need the door opened for them. Sometimes people need the handholding to get to the spot where they can go in and look. John got to the tomb first. He was there to encourage Peter. He was there to support Peter if Peter needed it.

> *In your darkest hour, in your moment of doubt, there must be a moment of confrontation.*

Think of some time when you were afraid. Maybe when you were little and you were frightened to go into a dark room, or to get on a roller coaster or to sit on Santa Claus's lap for the first time. Having your mother or your father there, or even having another child with you—your brother or sister, or a little friend holding your hand as you went up to that man with the big red suit—made it seem all right. Having them there gave you strength.

But they didn't get on the swing. You did. You had them there to help, but you did it for yourself. You confronted your fear.

Intervention can serve as a prelude to confrontation. But the intervention cannot serve as the be-all and end-all. At one moment in life, you're going to need to confront your fears, your addictions, and your problems for yourself.

In your darkest hour, in your moment of doubt, there must be a moment of confrontation.

Every recovering alcoholic and every recovering drug addict says the same thing: "I had to hit rock bottom." Now, rock bottom may be different for different people, but every addict says they hit their darkest hour, and then they realized *they* needed to confront whatever it was that took them there. It had to be them who realized it, so that it would be them who did it.

It is always darkest right before dawn. And that's the perfect time to confront what led you to that depth of darkness.

Chapter 23

Spiritual Warfare

I wholeheartedly believe that we have to go through a sort of process in order to experience the path of miracles that I believe exists for each and every one of us. That's life: process, process, process—journey, guideposts, meters, metrics. They're all outlined for us.

This whole thing of instantaneous gratification, of instant results and rewards—it doesn't work! Lottery tickets. No. Overnight sensations? They've been practicing, sweating, learning and trying since they were kids. Hollywood star discovered in a shopping mall? What took her there? She'd been running in the dark until she got to the point where she could walk through that mall at exactly the right moment, looking exactly right.

So what is the process?

First, we all must confront spiritual warfare. Paul talks about it in his Epistle to the Ephesians. He says the fight is "not against flesh and blood." It's "against the spiritual forces of wickedness." And we have to "put on the full armor of God," and "take up the shield of faith"[1]

There must be some sort of spiritual warfare before we experience our miracle. In that marathon there will be a moment when you begin to become dehydrated and you're going to have to refresh yourself, you're going to have to hydrate yourself. There is a moment of confrontation coming.

> *We have to confront the things that oppose us so we can reach what God has for us.*

---

1 Ephesians 6:11–24.

Why must there be confrontation? Why can't I just have all the blessings from the day I am born? Why must there be confrontation if I've believed strongly all the way from the beginning to the end? Why must I be challenged that way?

Because, first of all, there is a reality, and the reality is that we are not in Eden anymore. We are not in heaven. This is not a Pollyannaish existence. There are laws laid out as a result of the sinful nature of man, as a result of natural law. There is good and bad. There is good and evil. There is an antagonistic force that wants to stop you and me from reaching what God wants us to reach. There is opposition to your journey. There is opposition to your Third Day, your day of resurrection. There is opposition to your set of life-changing principles. There is opposition off the bat.

So the first thing we have to do on our journey is to confront the things that oppose us so we can reach what God has for us.

From the moment we're born there is opposition. Some who are reading this would say, "Okay, you're saying there is the diabolical, the devil."

But, hey, I have news for you: the opposition is even within ourselves. Because we are in this dichotomous existence. We have both the Kingdom Culture DNA embedded in our spirit and we have our Flesh Person, the outer person. That's the person we are confronting. That's the one who doubts. The one who falls. The one who curses. The one who fails. The one with nightmares and not dreams.

I confront that person every day. We have to understand from the get-go that this confrontation is continuous. Our job every day is to crucify that person. My challenge every day is to say, "What is the first thing I'm going to do? Crucify that person."

I will not be my number-one obstacle. I will not be my number-one hindrance. I will not be my number-one impediment. I will not be the reason why I did not succeed. I will crucify the Flesh Person—and put on the "new man," in the words of St. Paul.[2]

How do I do it? By faith. I activate that faith genome. I acknowledge the fact that there is a higher force, a higher power, a higher authority, who enables me to crucify that man and who tells me, "If you depend on me, I will give you the ability, the strength, the courage, the wherewithal, to live your life victoriously."[3]

---

2 Romans 6:6.
3 Mark 9:23; Philippians 4:13; Matthew 19:26; Jeremiah 17:7; Proverbs 16:20.

Prayer is the foundational platform. If we have different platforms—if we have a communicational platform, if we have a visionary, prophetic platform in seeing things that are not here yet—then prayer is the foundational communicational platform for each of the seven principles.

In order to activate each of these principles, you have to pray. You activate them by prayer.

Praise and worship and acknowledgment of God's sovereignty enable you to step into His authority and activate Kingdom Principles. As the Bible says, "enter His gates with thanksgiving, and His courts with praise."[4]

Equip yourself daily.

Equip yourself daily. That's what the Bible says: Renew your mind daily because the great battlefield of our existence is in the human mind.[5] It exists in our mind, in the thoughts that we have, and the ideas that we hold.

If I combine my thoughts with what verbally comes out of me, it will determine the outcome of my day. Those two things will combine and multiply and act together to determine the outcome of that day, because my actions are a consequence of both my thought process and my verbal affirmation.

Very few people act without thinking, even though some seem to be acting without thinking. They think, they do. We think, and the thought forms into words, and the words make that thought concrete. Whether they are spoken aloud, or spoken internally, silently. They give it form. They give it power. Our words send our thoughts into the physical world where they can take shape and become real.

Even if we don't want them to.

I can have good thoughts or bad thoughts. And I can send them out into the world through my words and actions. So I have to be sure the ones I send out are good, not bad. I have to confront those thoughts. I have to defeat that Flesh Man who undermines me, the one who doesn't let me focus on the future, and I have to help the inner man who wants to build the Kingdom Culture here on Earth.

---

4   Psalm 100:4.
5   2 Corinthians 10:4–5.

So it's confrontation first, then there's revelation and then there's activation and then saturation in that marathon of miracles.

Let me explain that.

The confrontation occurs first. I'm going to have to confront my outer man, that Flesh Man, and let my inner man, the Spirit Man, come out.

Then I have to confront whatever opposing forces may be out there in the world. Whatever it may be that's out there that's trying to hold me back, or that's trying to steer me in the wrong direction, or that's trying to cause me to fail. Because if I'm surrounded by people who live in their outer man rather than their inner man it's going to be a difficult journey. If they're going to continually be around me they're going to hold me back.

I need to surround myself with people who are not going to kill my dream. I want dream weavers, not dream killers. I need to be surrounded by people who are going to speak prophetically into my life. In other words, I need to be surrounded by people who are going to actually enrich my narrative, rather than bring it down.

> *Surround yourself with dream weavers, not dream killers.*

Those dream weavers are my helpers. They're my supporters. They can help me face the forces that oppose me. But they can't do it for me. It's up to me to confront those forces. If I don't do it myself, there will be no revelation.

Confrontation precedes revelation. Confrontation comes first, then comes revelation. Revelation means a truth is exposed. You find out that there is a miracle waiting for you—not only a miracle, but a series of miracles.

That revelation is the moment when you have learned the true meaning of the following phrase from divinity:

"Be still and know that I am God."[6]

I can be running and still be still. I can be running toward that goal, yet being still in knowing that God is God; knowing that even though I am running, God is working on my behalf. That He is doing things for me.

That's the revelation. When you really, truly, totally get that, there is rev-

---

6 Psalm 46:10, American Standard Version.

elation. There is understanding. There is knowledge and acknowledgment, discovery and perception.

That allows for activation, where specific God-given genes are activated. Activation is where Kingdom rules and Kingdom ways—Kingdom Culture—flow through me and around me. Where my way and His ways are one and the same, where I live by His rules fully in every aspect of my life. Where I do unto others not only as I would have them do unto me, but as He would unto us all.

And when I do that, after confrontation and revelation and activation, then comes saturation, which means that everything around me becomes an atmosphere of miracles. In other words, I am able to connect heaven to Earth—"on Earth as it is in Heaven."[7]

Have you ever been around someone who seems to just be hitting on all cylinders all the time? Someone who always seems to be getting it all right? It's pretty amazing. They seem to be blessed in whatever they do. Whatever they touch turns to gold.

Why is that? Because they've tapped into it. They've recognized that you have your own Kingdom personal atmosphere, and you can create a spiritual atmosphere with what you do. With what you believe. With what genes you activate. With what spirits and what you confront. With what is revealed. With what is saturated.

They've tapped into the reality that allows them to create their very own spiritual atmosphere. And you can, too. Through confrontation, revelation, and activation you achieve saturation, and you can actually transform your spiritual atmosphere. You can shift the atmosphere so that you, too, will be constantly blessed—and showered with blessings.

---

7 Matthew 6:10.

Principle Three

God Programmed Us to Have Partners

Chapter 24

SPIRITUAL DNA

What we see in the physical world is a direct reflection of what already exists in the spiritual world. Meaning that even within our DNA, as we analyze the mitochondria of the human genome, the strains and the strands that are there that carry who we are within them—our habits, our inclinations, our proclivities—we similarly have a Spiritual DNA. It's part of our programming. Regardless of who we are, it's there.

> *God's Spiritual DNA is alive in my life.*

There is a God who is bigger than us, and He has already deposited a piece of Himself in us. His Spiritual DNA exists in each and every one of us. That Spiritual DNA connects us to Him, and makes us act and think and behave the way we do in the same way that our parents' DNA makes us human.

It makes us *what* we are; but we make us *who* we are.

I can try to live in a way that goes against my Spiritual DNA, just like I could try to live in a way that goes against my human DNA. Instead of walking upright like a man, I could crawl around on all fours. But it would be unnatural, painful, and cause me permanent damage. If I live that way long enough, I could end up deformed, and I would never know the fullness and joy of life the way it was meant to be.

The same thing happens with my Spiritual DNA. I can live counter to it. I can ignore God's Kingdom Principles. I can let my Flesh Man rule over my Spirit Man. But I will cause myself pain and suffering, and, if I stay that way long enough, I might never know the fullness and joy of life the way God meant for it to be.

God made a deposit, and the deposit is alive in my life. And every single day that I activate God's genes inside me, I get closer to God. That's not making me "into" God, but activating the Spiritual DNA that He deposited inside of my being, inside of my Spirit Man, so that I can live the way He wanted me to.

The Spiritual DNA carries the genes that shape us and form our nature. We have faith and hope genes, and a mercy gene. We have a justice gene, and the genes that carry love. We have joy, peace, patience, meekness, goodness, gentleness, and temperance genes.

All of that is in us when we're born. It's already there when we come into the world.

Therefore, we're born to have faith. We are born prepared to believe what we cannot see, and to have conviction in what we hope for.

We are born to make sure the next generation does better than ourselves. We have embedded within us a commitment to making sure that our children do better than us. Not only do we want to make sure that our children do better than us, we want to make sure we leave a better Earth for our children than the one we received. We want to be sure that we leave behind more than we take. We want to make sure we pass the baton on to our children, and continue our heritage of hope and of faith and of doing good. And if we're successful at that we can connect the generations: the past, present, and future.

Faith triggers belief; belief triggers worship.

Activating any one of those genes activates other similar genes. The faith gene, if it's nurtured, has the power to activate the genes that give us hope and push us to accomplish. Faith triggers belief; belief triggers worship.

I think it's self-explanatory and self-evident. That's why most of the world believes in God, or in some sort of "God" or some sort of spiritual higher power. We were born to worship. And, because we were, we are going to worship something in life, regardless of who we are: it's either going to be money or God or something else. We're going to find something to worship. Regardless of who we are or what religion and inclination we have. We will find something to worship because we're worshippers.

Try to remove that. It's very difficult. It's embedded within our Spiritual DNA.

For the same reason, as children of God, regardless of whatever faith or religion we may call our own, we are inclined to believe. All of humanity is inclined to believe. We are even propelled to believe in the impossible, and in our ability to make the impossible possible.

That sort of belief—in what can be, that our dreams can come true, and in our own ability to make it happen—is what catapults us to reach the stars. It is that faith that catapults us to attain the great achievements mankind has accomplished throughout these thousands of years.

That faith propels us to survive against the odds. We are situated strategically and we have a propensity, when all things come against us, to survive. We are predisposed to come out of difficult circumstances. We are predisposed to survive tragedy. It is a God-given gene, a God-given spiritual reality within our Spirit Man. When God blew that breath of life into us, He deposited His Spiritual DNA within us. It is the life of God inside of us. As the Bible says: "the kingdom of God is within you."[1]

---

1   Luke 17:21.

Chapter 25

LIFE SURROUNDED

J esus knew the importance of partnerships. When he created his dream team, I imagine that he said, "I am going to create a team that's going to continue this revolutionary message of forgiveness and of hope and salvation and grace. I am going to bring together a team to spread this revolutionary message of forgiving those who have offended you. Of peace everlasting. Of joy. Of justice. Of taking care of those who cannot take care of themselves."

What a great message! It is a great, revolutionary message.

So he said, "I'm going to transfer it on. I'm going to make sure it lives on not just for a decade, not for a generation, but forevermore, if I'm successful. I'm going to make sure that all humanity is impacted by this message."

But he knew that the power of the message wasn't enough. He knew that the words alone wouldn't do it. The words needed voices to spread them. And he knew he couldn't do it alone. Of course, he knew he wasn't going to be around, alive and on Earth, for very long. So he knew he needed others to carry the message forward after he was gone. He understood the need for strategic partnerships.

So, he said, "I'm going to choose my team."

> *We live a Life Surrounded, exactly the same way that Jesus did.*

I don't think it is a coincidence that Jesus picked the twelve individuals he did. I don't think they were random choices. Jesus lived surrounded, on purpose. The twelve apostles he surrounded himself with, each had distinct characteristics. He chose them each for that specific reason, to fill a specific spot with their specific trait.

Thomas, of course, brought doubt; and Judas, betrayal. Peter stood for fear and denial; and John, for faithfulness. Andrew exemplified loyalty; James, security; Philip, commitment; Bartholomew, strength; Matthew, the tax collector, discipline; and James the Younger, of Alphaeus, honor. Jude showed compromise; and Simon, jealousy.

Each of these descriptors comes from their own personal narratives according to history. Much of that history is embedded within Scripture. Some of it exists beyond Scripture in different historical documentation, particularly in that of the Roman Empire.

I started teaching about Life Surrounded in leadership presentations in 2000, based on a careful analysis of each of the disciples. We looked at their lives and asked, what is their number-one contribution to the early church?

Even more important, we looked at the convergence of the life of Christ plus the individual contributions of each of these to try to answer the question, why would Christ pick these twelve? What's the motivation and what's the macro message for humanity in respect to a life surrounded by these individuals and what they each represent?

Did we make any assumptions? I believe not. We looked at how they lived with Christ; how they lived after Christ; and how they died, the end of their journey.

Then we took a look at what they did professionally. For example, Peter was a fisherman, someone who worked with his hands, was self-reliant, and who was, out of necessity, attuned with nature. Matthew was a tax collector. We know Matthew through his writings and through those of the other apostles.[1]

We understand Matthew from the narrative, and we understand his discipline as a tax collector—his due diligence, his detail, his commitment and his focus on details.

> *Christ was surrounded by these things—both negative*
> *and positive—and so are we.*

---

1 Matthew 9:9; Mark 2:14; Luke 5:27.

We also looked at who they spoke to after Christ's death. Matthew spoke to the Jews, Mark to the Romans, Luke to the Greeks, and John to the church. And later, Paul is sent to the Gentiles.

So we did all that in compiling their personality profiles and circumstantial profiles. That's how we created the rubric. That's how we found that one represents commitment, another honor.

I am convinced that these surroundings not only facilitated the platform for the success of Christ, but also were important to his success. He thrived in the midst of them—in spite of them, and because of them.

That's why I believe the message of Christ and the disciples speaks so powerfully.

Each of their histories gives us an abridged definition, or provides us an understanding that just as Christ, the embodiment of life, was surrounded by these things—both negative and positive—so are we.

We live a Life Surrounded, exactly the same way that Jesus did.

Somewhere in our lives we are going to have a Peter. Somewhere in our journey we are going to have a John. But somewhere in our journey we are also going to have a Thomas—and even a Judas.

Each of these individuals speaks to our lives today, about how relationships and people who impact our lives play a definitive role whether or not the mission and purpose in our lives is ever accomplished.

And all of them are necessary. Even the denier and doubter became great tools for success. They can be converted, and they can convert. None can be ignored, or left out. All of the places in our Life Surrounded group need to be filled. They all guide us, assist us, and help us learn by playing exactly the roles that Jesus knew they would.

We all have a Thomas. Somewhere in your life, in my life, we will meet someone who will not believe us for what we say but who will need to see the scars to prove that we've been through our journey. One of the people in our lives will doubt us. But there's a vitally important reason for that: that doubt will help me succeed. That doubt will push me to be accountable and to prove myself definitively. It will make me be more sure of myself and of what I have done, and it will make me capable of producing the evidence—through documents, through my track record, through what people say about me, or simply through my actions—to remove any doubt about what I have done and what I can do.

And I believe that somewhere in our journey we're all going to have a Judas. If not a Judas, a Judas moment, either a person or a moment of betrayal. And it could be self-inflicted, by the way.

> *We thrive in the midst of our Life Surrounded.*

Every single person will have a Thomas person or moment; a Peter person or moment; a John person or moment; and a Judas person or moment, a moment when you'll betray your core beliefs. A moment when you're betrayed or someone betrays you. A moment when that dream is betrayed, when the desire and the ambition is betrayed.

The betrayal comes from a lack of acknowledgment. From not acknowledging that God has purpose for your life. From not acknowledging the inevitable.

And, hard as it may be to accept or understand, this, too, the betrayal, is necessary. It leads you where you must go to follow the path of miracles.

Even the great leaders throughout history spoke to the notion of betrayal. From Alexander the Great, Hammurabi, and Napoleon to Plato, Aristotle, and Socrates—all spoke of betrayal, even prior to the Judas narrative. That idea of betrayal resonates from day one. Think of Adam and Eve in the garden.

The message is: You will be surrounded by doubt. You will be surrounded by denial. You will be surrounded by those who will surround you with love and care like John. You will be surrounded by all these circumstances. But you also will be surrounded by betrayal. Betrayal is not that far away. Betrayal will be close to you.

We're surrounded by faithfulness, and we're also surrounded by desire; we're surrounded by commitment, but we're also surrounded by betrayal. We're surrounded by honor, but we're also surrounded by denial. All of these things. We have our doubters, and our unwaveringly faithful. We have all these things in our life, just like Jesus did.

Discerning their characters, knowing their natures, and identifying their archetypes will help you recognize who these people are in your life—knowing which apostle is represented by each of the people surrounding you helps you identify their characteristics and their roles in helping you on your journey. Because of these people who surround us, and the roles they fulfill, we can discover the correct path for our journey and find the rewards God has waiting for us.

Chapter 26

REPLACING THE JUDAS IN YOUR LIFE

We all know that person, that woman or man, who never seems to have any "luck" in love. Time after time, every time, their relationships go sour. None of them ever seems to work out.

That person might even be you.

I have news for you: It doesn't have to be that way. You are not doomed to being alone. You are not condemned to never having that soul mate you long for by your side. Just the opposite. God meant for us all to have partners in life.

Don't give up. If you find yourself in that next relationship and that one goes bad, and the one after that goes bad, you still have to have faith. You must let the faith of God carry you along to know that right around the corner, literally, right around the corner, you will have your season of miracles.

But, before that can happen, you have one more responsibility. You can't just run in the same way to the same place over and over again. That's like running into the same spot on a brick wall over and over again. You might eventually wear it down and break through. But it's much more likely to break you.

It's the old saying: If at first you don't succeed, try, try again. Then find another way to do it. Otherwise, you're being foolish.

You can't just run in the same way to the same place over and over again.

The truth is, the ones who succeed are modifying their approach every time they try. You just may not notice. A high jumper who misses his mark the first time doesn't jump *exactly* the same way the next time. He jumps a little higher, pushes off a little harder, launches a little earlier, changes his approach angle. He does all of the above in different combinations or all together. He doesn't do it the same way again and again, hoping for a different outcome. And he doesn't give up.

Albert Einstein said that to do the same thing over and over again and expect different results is the definition of insanity. You must modify your modality. If the key you're using doesn't unlock the door, try a different key. If you use the same one over and over again, in exactly the same way, you already know what's going to happen. It won't open the door. It can't.

Your life, your job, your relationships, and your rewards work in exactly the same way. If you do exactly the same thing you're going to get exactly the same result. Finding another man who mistreats women, who doesn't know how to value the person at his side, who doesn't know how to cooperate, appreciate, or elevate the person he is with—or doesn't want to!—is going to end up exactly the same way as the last bad relationship you had.

> *If the key you're using doesn't unlock the door, try a different key.*

The problem is that even when we know that, even when we realize we need to clean that virus out of our hard drive, remove that bug from our program, and reinstall our software, we don't. We think we do, but we don't do a complete uninstall. We overlook a key element.

Here's the secret: something happened between the empty tomb and the upper room. Very, very few pastors, clergy, or ministers cover this. But, between the empty tomb and the upper room—between the place and time where Peter and John discovered Christ's body was gone and the place and time where Jesus appeared and all the apostles witnessed their miracle—one little incident with definitive repercussions took place:

Judas was replaced.

Between the empty tomb and the upper room the disciples got together and said, "Look, we're going to have to replace the one who betrayed Christ. Let's have an election."

And they did. They prayed, asking God to tell them who to pick. Then they picked straws and they chose, and Matthias was selected to replace Judas.

Judas was gone. But they didn't leave his place empty. And they didn't replace him with another Judas. They replaced him with someone better. They replaced him with someone different. They replaced him with someone who wasn't a betrayer.

What they did, you, too, must do. You must replace the betrayer in your life. You cannot leave that space empty. Whatever area in your life was betrayed must be replaced and not left void. But it has to be filled with someone better.

Once you know who that Judas is in your life, once you've identified the Judas DNA, you need to be mature enough to create a firewall. You need to put up a shield to prevent Judases from ever entering your life again. You don't have to keep going back to a betrayer.

But every empty space needs to be filled.

Every empty space will be filled eventually. It may not be with my first choice. It may not be with something that is helpful or efficacious. But it will be filled. And if you don't fill it with a good choice, you're leaving it open to be filled by someone or something that may not be any better—or may possibly even be worse—than what was there before.

You don't have to let that happen. And you don't have to repeat the same mistake. There is a difference between removing the betrayer from your life and removing him and replacing him with someone better.

Chapter 27

THE PRINCIPLE OF TWO BY TWO

We are created by God to do things in teams, never to do things by ourselves. To do things in partnerships. We're made to couple. To love.

It's part of our Spiritual DNA. The Good Lord in His creation made us predisposed to run in the dark, and He made us predisposed to have partners, to do things with someone else, never by ourselves.

Solitude and loneliness is not a God thing. It's the antithesis to what God intended. From day one, we are predisposed to do things with someone else, never by ourselves.

It's God's Principle of Two by Two: We are meant to be together, do things together, work together, and succeed together. We may go off alone, as Christ did, to make major decisions. And, we should, as he did, ask for guidance and instruction from Our Father. But once our mind is made up, we need to share our plan with our partners. God intends for us to partner with others in this world.

Consider Noah. When we say Two by Two, the first simple reaction is that we think of him. And that's correct. God spoke to Noah, and told him to build the ark. And He told him he was going to bring all the living things of the world into it. But he also told Noah to bring his wife and his sons, and his sons' wives aboard. He spoke to Noah in solitude, but He didn't want him to stay alone. He told Noah to get his partners—his wife and sons and daughters-in-law—and to be fruitful, and multiply.[1] The story of Noah and the Ark speaks to partnership's survivability. It's preventative, not reactive. It's securing in the ark what we want to have survive.

The same is true in our lives. We must secure within the confines of our

---

1 Genesis 7, 8, and 9.

destiny and our future what we want to survive. Regardless of how difficult the form of the flood may be, we must put in those partnerships. Two by Two guarantees continuity. It secures the viability of longevity, of heritage, even legacy. It is the continuation of DNA.

> *We are meant to be together, do things together, work together, and succeed together.*

Many of our failures can be attributed to the fact that we have done things by ourselves when we should have been in strategic partnerships. We must look at partnerships as our first choice, not our second choice. We should not look at partnerships as "let me try to do it by myself and if I fail then let me surround myself with the people or let me engage in partnerships or in collaborative relationships that will guarantee me success."

That's an erroneous way of thinking. It's not biblical. It's not divine. It's not God. It's not Kingdom.

We can see that that's true from day one. Let's look at the Genesis story. God believes that His relationship with Adam would suffice for Adam. Yet even then, the Bible says that Adam was lonely.

Now that's pretty difficult to justify theologically. How can you be lonely when you're walking with God? But there were some other needs that stemmed from this creation of God, from this thing called man. The Bible reveals an intrinsic truth: Man was never meant to be alone.

We limit that usually to the notion of marriage and to the notion of relationship with the opposite sex. But I want to go way beyond that. I want to go to the moment when we understand that we need to have partnerships in absolutely everything we do in life. That's been true throughout history: Adam and Eve, Elijah and Elisha, Peter and John.

Look at business models. Look at the Fortune 500 companies. Look at corporations around the world. Look at how many of them were at the brink of failure until they reached out and they merged with another company.

How many of the richest and most powerful corporations in the world have succeeded only via the avenue of mergers and acquisitions? How many would not be around today?

Because that's the reality: We need strategic partnerships, not as a second choice, but as a first choice principle. Not as an afterthought. Not, "Let me try things on my own and if I fail then I'm going to merge and partner with someone else." Strategic partnerships guarantee continuity. They guarantee the continuation of the line. They protect us. Regardless of the flood or the storm, if two work together, that type, that class, will survive. Survivability is a consequence of partnership.

So a strategic partnership is defined as that person who can bring strengths in your areas of weakness. Who can help push you when you are flagging. Who has skills you may not have. And perhaps has some skills that you do have that when combined give more force. That's the way it works in business.

> *We need strategic partnerships, not as a second choice,*
> *but as a first choice principle.*

It's not new. And it's not just in the Bible. We have had great partnerships throughout history. The bringing down of the Berlin Wall, the end of the Cold War, it was Reagan and Gorbachev. Reagan by himself—which he himself admitted, by the way—would never have succeeded. It was through a partnership. We're not talking about what degree of support they each provided. We're not saying who did more than the other, who put in more effort, to reach that goal. But there is no question that it was through their partnership that they accomplished it. Neither one could have done it alone.

In the same way, Winston Churchill and Franklin Delano Roosevelt aligned themselves with Josef Stalin, the communist despot, to defeat Hitler. Our democratic nations worked together in partnership with the communists to stop the spread of fascism. And it was that partnership that brought victory. Any one of them working alone could have resulted in a very different—and possibly very frightening—outcome to World War II. They saw that. They saw that to stop the massive Nazi war machine, they needed to come together, in concert.

It's true on a global scale such as that, and it's true in your personal world. There are things you can do alone, but you can always accomplish more working with others.

A musician can play beautifully alone. But bring all the right musicians together, with the correct collection of instruments, and they can form an orchestra capable of playing wonderful and complex symphonies. It's impossible for one musician alone to accomplish that.

That's how it works. You can do marvelous things alone. You may do things that make a real difference in the world. But to truly change the world, you need to have partners.

When a brilliant cardiologist performs open-heart surgery that saves someone's life, the doctor gets the credit—as well he should. Without him, it wouldn't have happened. But he didn't do it alone. Every surgery involves a team. Without the anesthesiologist, the nurses, the assisting doctors, the technicians—without every one of the people in the operating room—that operation would never have succeeded.

That's what partnerships are all about. It's teamwork. It starts with two people coming together for a common goal. But it doesn't have to stop with two. No way! Those two are just the beginning. The team continues to grow, to six, eight, twelve—like the apostles—or twelve thousand. The Principle of Two by Two doesn't mean you have to stop at two; it means you need at least two. Two is just a starting number. The team grows to match the goal.

For a marriage, you need two. For a football team, eleven, at least. It took hundreds to build the Empire State Building, and thousands to put the first man on the moon.

How many does it take to change the world?

Jesus started with twelve.

> *There are things you can do alone, but you can always accomplish more working with others.*

Before he found and partnered with the twelve apostles, though, there was one other—one that we often take for granted; one that we often overlook. But it's the primary partnership every one of us should begin with. Before he formed his team, Jesus forged the principal partnership of his life: with God.

You should, too. The first partnership you should begin with, the one that should always be the primary partnership in your life, is with you and the divine. You and God. I would be audacious enough, courageous enough, to say that God *wants* to partner with you.

That's not part of the commonplace theology. Saying God wants to forge that partnership with you presents the underlying notion that God has a need. Why would God need to partner with us?

Well, God needs to partner with us because embedded within the law that he Himself created—His laws, His principles—we are the extension, the manifestation of God here on this planet.

If good occurs, if justice is revealed, it comes through the embedded DNA incorporated in each and every one of our beings. God is looking for people to partner with to transform families, homes, communities, nations. God wants to partner with us, and seeks to partner with us.

He's looking for people who are willing to adhere to His mandates and His principles, who want to build Kingdom Relationships, guided by Kingdom Principles—of love, joy, peace, faith, patience, meekness, goodness, gentleness, temperance, mercy.

All of those are embedded within us when we first come into the world. They are the fruit of the spirit. They are part of our Spiritual DNA.

Kingdom Relationships are healthy. They are advantageous mutually. They edify. They enrich, not only themselves and each other, but everything around them. And they make sure that those who follow are greater than ourselves.

> *The primary partnership is you and God.*

Chapter 28

GOD'S PARTNERS

God seeks partnerships in the twenty-first-century world. He seeks partnerships for a transformative purpose. He seeks partnerships to change lives, to transform lives, and to catapult each and every individual human being to their destiny and their prophetic purpose.

Like any good partner, God will help us overcome our obstacles, complete our tasks, and accomplish our goals. But God doesn't do it for us. That's the mistake people make—in the way they live and in the way they say their prayers. People expect God to do things for them.

When the storm hits, too many people say, "God, please, get me out of this." Whether it's a literal storm, with rain and lightning and rising waters and hail and gale-force wind, or a figurative storm—those financial storms, and marital storms, and career storms that batter and shake us, the ones we fear will break us—too many people ask God to lift them out of the stormwater, to lift them out of their financial problems, or to fix their relationships.

They're wrong.

I don't ask God to change my circumstances; I ask God to partner with me and help me change. So I can change. If not, I will repeat that circumstance again. We get to do it again and again until we learn the lesson that it's *us* changing, not the circumstances changing.

It's not: "God, get me out of this." It's: "Get this out of me."

When we get down on our knees and pray for God's help, when we ask for deliverance, we're thinking, "God, I'm going to use you to change my circumstances." That's not the way it works. It's the other way around. God says, "Actually, I'm going to use you."

We need to remember that God is not our tool. We're His.

> *Don't ask God to change your circumstances; ask God*
> *to help you change.*

We are to pursue partnership. And our number-one partnership should be with God.

In my case I realized He wanted me to be His partner when I was fourteen years old.

As I told you earlier in this book, I started praying to God every day from the time I was five. I believed I could speak to God, and that I could hear and see His answers in different ways—in nature, in my relationships, in things that happened to me.

But that was just me talking.

Then, when I was fourteen, I had an epiphany.

I was a freshman in high school, seeking God, wanting to do God's will. One night, it was ten-something. I had my little black-and-white television in my room. I turned it on and I saw a televangelist who was very popular at the time, saying, "There is a better day tomorrow."

It was just a clip. But as he spoke—and I'm willing to take a lie detector test and pass it successfully—I heard a still small voice in my heart that said, "Look at that. Look at what you're seeing. I'm going to take you to a place where you're going to be able to share the Good News and lives will be changed. I'm going to use you for that."

Then the clip ended. The program went to a commercial break and I changed the channel to PBS. That's what kind of a nerd I was. I loved PBS. So I changed the channel, and there was a special on about Martin Luther King Jr.

Now, when I was fourteen years old, he was one of my heroes. And I'm listening, and I saw the speech in Washington, the 1963 speech—the "I have a dream" speech. And, again, I hear a still small voice in my heart saying, "Do you see that? I'm going to do that with you. I'm going to raise you up as a voice for your people."

So I know God wants to partner with us.

But He doesn't want it to stop there. We also should be in strategic, collaborative relationships in what we do at home with our families, in our communities, and in our lives. God wants me to make more partnerships. In every aspect of my life. In all that I do. In every field and every area—in my business, in my home, in my community. Partnerships.

God wants us to wake up every single day and say, "Who will I partner with?" This very day. Not tomorrow or sometime in the future but today, right now: "Who will I partner with?"

Can I do that every single day? Can I wake up and know—not hope, or think, or suspect that it's true, but know—that this very day, God will provide for me a new partner?

Can I wake up asking myself: Who can I work together with this day, who will not only change my life and impact my life but who will assist me in my personal journey? Who can I partner with to transform our surroundings, the air and the environment? Who can I partner with to do good? Who can I partner with to achieve exceedingly, abundantly, above all?

It's true. I do it in my own life. Even within the organization I preside over we made sure from day one that everything we would do would be through partnerships. In everything we do.

Why reinvent the wheel? If someone else is actually doing what we want to achieve, let's partner with them—as long as we share the same core values. That's what provides the rubric for the partnership, the ground rules: shared core values. You must have shared core values.

> *God wants us to wake up every single day and ask, "Who will*
> *I partner with?" This very day.*

Before you go into a partnership, you must know your core values, and you must know what you are willing to compromise. That's the great question of partnerships: What are we willing to compromise? That's the sticky point of partnerships. What object am I willing to place on the altar? What am I willing to sacrifice? What am I willing to compromise?

I have to know that I'm going to make compromises, because we're going to work together as partners. I have to know that you may not run as fast as I can so I have to go a little bit slower. I have to know what I am I willing to give up, to surrender, to make concessions on. What is my variable rate? What is my variable component? What can I be flexible in?

But it is even more important for me to know what areas are absolutely untouchable. That's where we come back and say, "These are my nonnegotiables." Prior to agreeing to a partnership there must be clarity and transparency in our nonnegotiables. These are our nonnegotiables come hell or high water. On this field we will die.

We must be driven in our lives by nonnegotiables. What are the things I believe in that I will believe in for the rest of my life? That drive me? That are part of my DNA? That cannot be forgotten or ignored, regardless of what may happen? I may finesse it and massage it and there may be nuances that may occur that are different from the original, but these are the core values. And those core values are never compromised. Those core values are vital and critical to our success.

Chapter 29

PICKING YOUR RUNNING PARTNER

Whether you're changing the world or changing your life, you need a partner.

Even Jesus knew that. He knew he couldn't do it alone. And if he knew he couldn't, what could possibly make you think that you could?

The notion that we can run this journey in life by ourselves is wrong. It needs to be squelched. We need a running partner in life, just like Peter needed John.

But we have to be able to pick the right running partner. Because it's the relationships we forge that will either catapult us to our success or secure our failure. It is the partnerships that we create that will lead us to victory or condemn us to defeat. It is the associations we form that will lift us or crush us.

So your running partner, the person you want at your side, has to be someone who will run with you, not against you; someone who will help you on your journey, not prevent you from reaching your goal.

> *The notion that we can run this journey in life by ourselves is wrong.*

Why do we need running partners?

1. As a firewall. It acts as a security barrier.

Working with others acts as a firewall. It protects me from harm, the same way that a firewall in a car or a house does. It does exactly what its name says: it puts a wall between fire and me. Nowadays the same term is used with computers, and the intent remains the same: a firewall in a computer is a protective shield to keep intruders from harming my computer system.

That's what my running partners in life do, too. They help shield me from harm. They help me resist those people and things that would hurt me, weaken me, cloud my thinking (the way a hacker's bug in my computer system would do), and cause me to lose my way.

It is going to be more difficult to defeat two than to defeat one. The majority of crimes are committed against individuals who find themselves alone. Be it in their house, be it in their neighborhood, or be it in their car. Very few crimes are committed against groups of two or more. It is a deterrent to ill will, to evil.

2. If I fall I have someone immediately next to me, who will pick me up. It acts as a restorative mechanism. If one falls the other will be there to help, to lift, and to support. If one can't shoulder the burden, the other can take over; or they can share the weight between them. If one is blinded momentarily, or takes a wrong turn, the other can lead the way back to the right path. As the Bible says, "Two are better than one."[1] Because we do get lost sometimes. We do find ourselves misguided and misled, attracted to the glitter instead of to the light. And, when that happens, our partner can help us find our way again.

3. To compensate for my shortcomings. My running partner needs to be someone who has strength where I have weakness, and vice versa. My partner will be capable in the areas I have not mastered or demonstrated proficiency in. Someone who has faith when I have fear. We complement each other.

A pilot flies the plane, but he needs a navigator to guide him. The doctor needs a nurse. Your running partner's skills and your own need to mesh in a way that helps you both to succeed. The sum should be greater than the parts. In business school this is called "synergy" or $2 + 2 = 5$.

4. Partnership speaks to the heart of God. It speaks of God Principle. It speaks of the Father, the Son, and the Holy Spirit. It speaks of team, of collaboration.

That's why in the Bible it says, "If two or more come in agreement over

---

1   Ecclesiastes 4:9–11.

the one thing, I will be in the midst of that."[2] That means that if two or more pray together for the same thing—that's what "agreement" means in the Bible, to pray together—God will be there with them.

That's pretty amazing. If you pray with someone over the same thing, it's more leverage. The prayer of agreement comes from two. It's one thing to agree within yourself, but to agree with someone else is transformative. It has explosive potential. The amount of energy coming together creates a cathartic fusion. A spiritual fusion. A prophetic fusion.

We understand what happens when the atom is split. But over the last thirty years, we really have come to understand what happens when the atoms come together. And the amount of energy produced by the atoms coming together is amazing. Explosive. Unlimited.

Now, be informed: It's not a once-and-for-all partner.

There are specific people God brings our way. For a specific season. For a specific day. For a specific purpose.

Every day there's an opportunity for viable partnership. Every day I can collaborate with someone to do something great. And to fulfill not only my journey but also the corporate journey of this great brotherhood, of this great fellowship we call mankind.

We can transform this world. We can change the world through partnership. But only after we understand that around us we are surrounded by the traitors and doubters and deniers.

Remember, you live a Life Surrounded, just like Jesus, and you have to identify your partners, to know who they are and what their character is—are they Peters who will deny you, Johns who will believe in you totally, or Judases who will betray you? In order for me to identify my partner, I must identify who is surrounding me and understand that close to me I have doubt, I have betrayal, I have denial.

We are surrounded by those who deny, those who betray, and those who doubt. But we're also surrounded by the other nine. And they're not that bad. Not bad at all. We have faith and fellowship, discipline and honor. We have Thomas, Judas, and Peter, but we also have John, Andrew, and Matthew. We have the others.

Knowing who and what they are, you can minimize the damage of the

---

2 Matthew 18:20.

traitors and the deniers, and maximize the benefits of the loyal supporters and the doubters.

> *It's the relationships we forge that will either catapult us to our success or secure our failure.*

How do I do that? How do I not pick Judas when I'm looking for John?

Selection, selection, selection. There must be a rubric created to be able to measure, or to be able to identify which is the most viable partner.

We must learn to test their spirits, and we must remain alert so we can spot the cues that reveal the reality of their nature. We must apply our God-given spirit of discernment, that God-given genome to identify or to be able to distinguish between the truth and a lie.

It won't always be easy. Thomas, the doubter, may come up and let you know from the very beginning who he is. But the Judas in your life most likely won't introduce himself as the guy who is going to betray you. (And don't be thrown off if "he" is really a "she." As Samson well knows, the betrayer can just as easily be a woman.)[3] There is no way that person is going to shake your hand and say, "Hello, I'm the Judas in your life. I'm here to deceive you, cheat on you, and double-cross you."

Yes, it would be nice if every person you meet wore a huge sign that said, "Betrayer" or "Denier." But that's not the way it works. It's not supposed to. You'd think that would help, but it wouldn't. It would be counterproductive to the process of discovery on our journey through life.

Jesus knew who each of the apostles really was and what they were really like, but he also knew that they each played a necessary role. If we saw a betrayer coming our way, and we knew it from the outset, we'd be more likely to run the other way. And if we did that, we would never learn the lesson we're supposed to learn and we would never, ever—not in a million years—discover our purpose and find the rewards God has waiting for us.

Let's look at the history here. Let's look at the apostles, at their actions and their responses to definitive moments. They reveal themselves in ways

---

3 Judges 16:4–21.

we can all recognize and understand. Jesus knew, and we can, too—if we pay attention.

When the lady who Christ forgave brought her expensive perfume and she spilled it on the feet of Jesus, it was Judas who was perturbed by the fact and who spoke up. He said, "We could have sold this and used the money to fill our ministry coffers."[4] What he really was opposed to was not the excess use of the oil that could have been used for ministry purposes. What he was really opposed to was that lady's worship of Christ. He was jealous of her worship. Right then, right there, Judas demonstrated an envious spirit, similar to Lucifer.

He revealed himself right there. He showed his true colors.

You will recognize the Judases in your life the same way. They will show you who they are; you just need to keep your eyes open. You need to believe what you see and know, not what you wish to be true. A pig is a pig even if you paint wings on it. And painting wings on a man doesn't make him an angel.

> *You don't ever want to be surrounded by the pathetic. You want to be surrounded by the prophetic.*

I must surround myself with the people, with the players, with the partners I want in my life. I have to do what the author and business consultant Jim Collins would call identifying those who should be "on the bus."

Now these are not visitors. We need to be careful. We need to identify who are the visitors and who are the shareholders. Who will stay close? Who will have a stake in my journey, in my life? Who's going to own a piece of my heart?

I must identify, number one, those who agree—there must be kindredness of spirit. We have a destiny and a purpose given to us by God for us to live life to the fullest—exceedingly, abundantly, above all. The people I surround myself with must have similar goals. They must have similar values, and apply similar metrics.

---

4 Matthew 26:6–13.

In other words, I don't want to be surrounded by the "good enough" people in the world. I want to be surrounded by the "exceedingly, abundantly, above all" people. I want to be surrounded by people who believe in direction, not deception. I want to be surrounded by the people who are committed to those notions and ideas I am committed to—of DNA, of righteousness, of justice, of Kingdom Culture, of transferability to the next generation of family. Those are the people I want to surround myself with, those with the same Kingdom values as me.

You don't ever want to be surrounded by the pathetic. You want to be surrounded by the prophetic. You need to get away from those who are naysayers and deniers and doubters and traitors. Don't ever be surrounded by someone who will speak against your success and against your outcome. If you surround yourself with people who only speak negative into a circumstance, they will hinder you on your journey. They will hold you back. They will lead you to the shadows instead of the light, pull you toward the past instead of the future.

Surround yourself with those who celebrate your successes. Surround yourself with those who rejoice in your achievements. Surround yourself with those on the Path of Miracles.

Chapter 30

ACCEPTING FAILURE

We all have this intrinsic motivation when we fall that makes us want to get back up. But many don't. They can't; they won't; they don't know how. But deep down inside they want to.

The problem is that wanting to and actually succeeding are two different things.

So they turn to us for a hand. And we *think* we really want to help them. We really do. In our hearts, that is our intention. In our minds, that is what we believe. But in our actions, we hold them down.

We hold them down by accepting their failure. It's one of the most terrible things that we do in our lifetime. It's terrible for them and for us. It doesn't matter what the failure is. It could be a moral failure, an economic failure, a political failure. We do the, "Oh, I'm so sorry it happened!" The, "Oh, that's such a shame!" We have this sort of placating, even somewhat condescending, sort of demeanor and presentation and response mechanism: "It's a shame. My prayers are with you."

But the truth is, we catapult ourselves on those failures. We basically use them to justify our own shortcomings and say, "I'm not the worst of them." Or, "I'm not the least of them." We measure ourselves against the lowest bar.

Which is a shame. That speaks to our humanity rather than to the divinity. It speaks to our human, earthly, terrestrial inclination, rather than to our Kingdom Principles.

> *By helping others get up, we help ourselves rise higher.*

When we accept the failures of others, and use them as a step stool so we can feel better about ourselves, we are failing. That's not stepping up; that's stepping down. By helping others get up—and, even more important, helping them stand on their own—we help ourselves up; we rise higher.

We have a moral and a Kingdom responsibility to restore. We have a moral and God-given responsibility in partnership, because I'm not only in partnership in my personal journey, I'm in partnership with my brothers and sisters in mankind as God's children, the children of God's kingdom, the citizens of God's kingdom, that if one of mine fails, we must restore! Or at least do whatever we can to bring about a restorative process.

There must be a commitment to restore anyone around me in my life who falls—at least to try.

Of course, they have free will. They can accept or reject my inclination and my assistance. It can't be forced or coerced. But I am morally and biblically and Kingdom obligated to reach out and restore.

If you look at it as a team: How far can I get with someone on their knees when I'm running?

> *There must be a commitment to restoration through our partnership.*
> *That way, we all succeed.*

We're interconnected more than we realize. We understand this now more than ever in our global economy. In the age of globalization, our economies are completely interconnected. There is interdependency. Not just economically and politically. The days are gone when one nation can have an economic depression and the other nations not be impacted. One small nation, their deficiency in producing corn or rice produces what we have today as a food scarcity pertaining to rice and other products.

The flooding of the rice paddies in Vietnam impacts how much rice can be sold at Wal-Mart in the United States. This is globalization.

We are totally interconnected. We are connected with that young man, who through an Internet connection somewhere in Myanmar, in Burma, shows me pictures of the devastation following a typhoon. His struggle becomes my struggle. His pain becomes my pain. And if he falls I have a responsibility to see if somehow I can do anything beyond moral support to lift him up.

We are connected to the children in Haiti, suffering from malnutrition and ill from contaminated water. Their need is my need. Their illness is my illness. The Kingdom connection is a global connection; my connection to God requires me to connect with my fellow man. And if I don't, if I allow them to fall and make no effort to help them get back up again, then I fall with them.

There must be a commitment to restoration through our partnership. That way, we all succeed.

Chapter 31

COVENANT RELATIONSHIPS

We all know that woman or man who's been through a horrible relationship, or two, or three. It may even be you.

It seems they do the same thing over and over again, end up with exactly the same kind of person, and end up with the exact same result.

Or, after a few fumbles, after a few failures, they vow "never again!" And they run from any relationship. Their fear keeps them from getting close to anyone, and they go through life alone, and lonely.

There are three reasons.

First, they haven't confronted their fear. There's no moment of confrontation that leads to revelation that leads to activation that leads to saturation. None of that has occurred.

Second, they haven't applied any of the Kingdom Principles. They're still in a state of spiritual identity moratorium. They have no idea who they are spiritually. There is no notion of who they are as citizens of God's kingdom.

And, third, their validation and maintenance modality continuously survives on the behavior that they interpreted to be abusive. We know that psychologically many of them see it to be some sort of demonstration of affirmation.

They respond by doing one of two things. They either repeat the story again, or run from it. They either dance to the same tune or refuse to ever dance again—because there is no confrontation.

Confrontation is the exposing of truth. Confrontation for any other reason is violence. Confrontation should lead to the exposing of truth.

And we should be clear here that we're not looking for confrontation that leads to violence. We're looking for a spiritual confrontation—an intrinsic, motivational, emotionally exuberant, affective confrontation that will expose truth.

We want to expose God's glory in every single human life. We want to expose God's glory in every single relationship.

> *The power of two recognizing their purpose and coming together on their journey is infinite.*

So, if that person does not make you better, if that person does not facilitate and make you a new reality, if that person is a dream killer rather than a dream weaver, and if that person does not accept transformation, you need to separate from that person. If that person does not accept the God-given mandate to serve and to love and embrace rather than to harm and to crush dreams, you need to end your relationship and go on your way.

That kind of person is not a running partner. That kind of person helps make you stronger, yes. That kind of person helps you clear the clouds from your eyes and to see where your journey lies. But that is not someone to keep by your side.

God put them on your journey to help you realize what you need to do in life, to help make you stronger, to help show you where you do *not* want or need to be. And once you realize that, it's time to go.

Now, if they will accept transformation, if they will realize, recognize, understand, and acknowledge that they need to love and serve and embrace rather than to harm, then God may have put them in your journey so that you could help them. He may have put that person there so that you both become stronger and learn to become true running partners, and a true team.

And when those individual atoms come together as one, when those two strands of DNA weave together, watch out! Prepare for your daybreak! Because God knows that the power of two together is not just two *plus* two, it's two *times* two, and ten, and twenty, and two hundred. The power of two recognizing their purpose and coming together on their journey is infinite.

But how in the world do you find that person?

The natural reaction of someone coming out of a bad relationship might be, "Let me find someone who is the opposite of who I had. Here's my criteria, my measuring tool, my metrics for a new partner. And the first one is: I want someone totally the opposite of what I had."

We need to be careful in creating metrics based on our past experience.

We need to incorporate within our measuring system preventive mechanisms by conceptualizing the failures of the past. However, the past cannot be what drives us. Even the failures of the past. Even the wounds and the hurts and the bad relationships of the past should not drive us.

The selection process must be driven by the impetus of the future. The correct method is optimistic. It is positive. It is driven by the positive energy, and the vertical relationship and the horizontal consequence. It is driven by heaven and not by hell. It is driven by what God has for me rather than what the earth has for me. It's driven by where I'm going to rather than where I'm coming from.

> *The past cannot be what drives us.*

You still have to respect the fact that intrinsically there is a self-defense mechanism to make sure that we don't repeat the mistakes of the past. However, in selecting a partner, I'm not going to select a new partner by first answering the question, "Is this the opposite of what I had before?" The metrics need to be structured around the outcome. And the desired outcome is based on Kingdom Principles rather than earthly consequences.

The people who go back and repeat their behaviors and make their bad choices are not looking for someone who has the same core values. They haven't looked at themselves and asked, "What are those values I have that are nonnegotiable?"

One thing is nonnegotiable: I don't want this person around me who is going to belittle me and abuse me verbally or any other way. That's nonnegotiable.

Everything else is. My point is that other than the nonnegotiables, everything else is up for grabs. The rules of the game are: identify your nonnegotiables, the unwavering, I-won't-budge-on-these things; everything else is up for grabs. Everything else is open to compromise.

In other words, what I want is to continue to be proactive rather than reactive. We live in a world where most people change partners on a reactionary whim rather than having sufficient data through research and analysis to enable us and give us enough information to make a valid decision.

Let's look at the increase in multiple marriages. And by multiple, I mean not just divorced once, but the inclination to divorce again and again. If we look at the statistics, we understand that if you divorced once you're inclined to divorce again. Why? Because we continue to engage in this reactionary sort of metric: "Well, these are the things that this previous partner was deficient in." And, "That's another thing I'm looking for in this new partner."

Instead of looking at deficiencies, let's look at strengths. Let's look at complementary strengths.

There is a compatibility notion that needs to be measured in all of our partnerships. It's either going to reinforce something you already have or it's going to complement. The moment of angst occurs when it does neither of the above. When it confronts and it's a hindrance to one of your strengths. Someone else's strengths may be a hindrance to yours.

You definitely want to create a measuring system. You want to incorporate a system in your life where the partner you choose, with the proper prescriptive dynamics, is someone who can take you to the next dimension. Not to the next level, but the next dimension.

> *Instead of looking at deficiencies, look at complementary strengths.*

Does this person impact your atmosphere when they are around you, when they are in your life? Remember, it is the atmosphere that protects us against the external forces—the physical, emotional, and spiritual meteorites and comets and asteroids—that come our way. So, ask yourself, is this a person who crashes into your atmosphere and depletes it, disrupts it, or damages it?

Or is it someone who enriches your atmosphere?

Anyone in our lives has the potential of doing two things: they either impact you directly, or your atmosphere. Anyone. And every one of them can do good or harm.

We want to make sure that the partners with whom we establish what I would call a covenant, which is a biblical term for agreement—it is a pledge, a promise, a contract—are worthy of our trust.

The Principle of Covenant Relationship is the principle of reciprocity in spirit and in purpose, in passion and in promise.

The key word is reciprocity. It means to return in kind, that they behave the same way toward you as you behave toward them—with mutual respect, love, caring, understanding, and all the other positive qualities that a good and healthy relationship should include. Or, as Jesus put it: "Do unto others as you would have them do unto you."[1] Reciprocity means they do the same back.

In a covenant relationship, you hold mutual core values, you share a purpose, and you support each other in any individual goals. Your passion is reciprocated, and you both keep your promises to each other.

From that foundation you both can grow together, and so can your love for each other.

---

1 Matthew 7:12.

Chapter 32

DREAM WEAVERS AND
DREAM KILLERS

The what, where, when, and why are not as important as the who. It's the who that matters first. Who leads the way. How, why, when, where, and what follow.

Usually, we have it the other way around. We live life, and we incorporate the opposite of this principle. Let's say I want to start a business that deals with digital platforms or Web site creation, that incorporates both the blogosphere and audiovisual. It's like the nexus of YouTube with MySpace with a blog, all in one. That's what I'm going to do.

In the usual modus operandi I ask myself, "Okay, now what resources do we have? What's it going to cost? What's the initial capital investment? Do I have any venture capitalists I can speak to?"

In reality, I would put all that away. Strike that. Remove it. Take that away from the table.

> *Who's on your team? That's what's important.*

Instead of putting down, "*What* do you want to do?" the first question should be, "*Who* are you going to work with?"

Who's on your team? That's what's important. Who are you surrounding yourself with? Have you identified the faithful? The disciplined? The doubter who will force you to quality-test your ideas, to research and field-test so that you know you have the evidence to back your presentation?

First, who; then, what.

There are people you can partner with regardless of your dream. They have the DNA to take your dream and make it a reality regardless of what it may be. They can partner, facilitate an environment, create a culture, create an atmosphere. These are dream weavers. These are people who God brings your way to help make your dream a reality.

God puts dream weavers along your path so that you can join together and find your purpose and your mission together—then you will realize your true dream. You may have a dream now, and you may make that dream come true along the way, but your true dream, the ultimate goal, the dream that matches your purpose and your mission, will become clear to you *after* you connect with your team of dream weavers. And that dream can become a reality only after you make someone else's dream come true.

This is the Kingdom process of dreams. We begin with having a dream. That's step one. Second, we begin interpreting other people's dreams for them. Third, we serve someone else's dream—we make someone else's dream come true.

Our dream will never become a reality until we make someone else's dream a reality first. Make someone else's dream come true and you will see your dream become a reality. The reason why so many people never see their dream materialize is because they've never served someone else's dream.

> *Our dream will never become a reality until we make someone else's*
> *dream a reality first.*

There's a biblical narrative to support this, from the life of Joseph. It's what I call a pit-prison-palace journey.[1]

Joseph began having dreams.[2] As a matter of fact, he had a dream that his brothers would all serve him. But Joseph jumped the gun. Joseph shared the dream with his brothers ahead of time. And his brothers were just indignant about it: "What do you mean we will serve you?"

They also didn't like the fact that Joseph's father had given him a multicolored robe. The robe represented the favor of his father. And Joseph's

---

1 Genesis 37–50.
2 Genesis 37:5–8.

brothers became envious of him. So his brothers took away Joseph's robe, and they placed him in a pit.

There's the first lesson: We have to be very careful who we share our dreams with. Because if we share our dream with the wrong people, they may want to strip us of that dream. These are dream killers.

Anyway, Joseph was left in the pit, but he never lost his dream. Because we can lose our robe, we can lose the trappings and we can lose the material wealth and the things that we gained that we worked for, but there is something that we can never lose—our dream.

There are things that life and our enemies can take away, but there are things they cannot. In our pit moments, life and circumstances and our enemies—spiritual, physical, or otherwise—may take away our happiness, but not our joy; they may take away our house, but not our home; they may take away our money, but not our riches; and they may take away our past, but definitely not our future.

They can take away one but not the other because one of them is earthly and the other is eternal. One is physical and worldly, and the other is divine and Kingdom. The only one who can take it from us is God, because He gave it to us.

> *If we share our dream with the wrong people, they may want to strip us of that dream. These are dream killers.*

Joseph proved it. In the midst of that pit, Joseph still had his dream. And when they pulled him out of the pit and sold him into slavery, he still had his dream.

But even after he got out of the pit, he wound up in prison!

After he got out of the pit, he became one of Potiphar's slaves. Potiphar was the captain of Pharaoh's bodyguards, and he bought Joseph and put him to work in his house. Potiphar liked Joseph. And, eventually, he made Joseph his overseer, in charge of everything in his house and everything he owned.

Everything was going along smoothly—Joseph did well, and Potiphar did well, and Potiphar's house did well under Joseph's supervision—until Joseph got into a little situation with Potiphar's wife.

Potiphar's wife wanted to have sex with Joseph. Or, as they put it in the Bible, she kept trying to get him to "lie down" with her. Joseph tried to get away. She grabbed his clothes and held on, and, as he ran off, he wound up naked.

(If Joseph were alive today we probably would have accused him of having some sort of sexual deviancy, of being some sort of quasi-perv. Everywhere Joseph went he ended up buck-naked—his brothers stripped him, for crying out loud! Then he goes to Potiphar's house and Potiphar's wife strips him and leaves him naked. We would put Joseph on a couch today and find out what's really going on here! However, that's a sermon for another time.)

Anyway, Potiphar's wife called out, and, as a result, Joseph goes to prison.

In prison, Joseph meets a baker and a butler—chief baker and cupbearer are their official titles in the Bible. But by the time Joseph meets them he no longer cares about his dream. He no longer articulates his dream. He doesn't walk into prison and say, "Aha! I want you to know that one day everyone is going to serve me." He forgets about that sort of presentation.

Now his commitment is to interpret other people's dreams.

The baker and the butler each had a dream and told Joseph about it, and he gave them each their interpretation. For the butler, Joseph saw good news. In three days, he said, the Pharaoh would release him from prison and give him his old job back. But in three days, Joseph said, the baker would die.

Why does the baker die and the butler live? Because if you build your own kingdom, if you build your own fame without serving, you and your dream will die. He who served, lived. He who built for himself and not to serve others, died. The baker built his business for himself. The butler, literally, served others.

Whatever we build in life, if it does not serve the greater good of others, if it does not serve a greater cause, it will die. Regardless of what it may be. If it does not serve a greater cause, it will die. And, if it serves a greater cause, it will thrive.

Joseph will prove that himself, too, but a couple of years go by first. That's important to remember. Because when the butler was released from prison and went back to work for his old boss, Joseph told him to please,

"Remember me to Pharaoh." I'm sure Joseph was hoping to get out of prison himself and thought it would be good to have friends in high places. After all, he had done the butler a favor by interpreting his dream.

But the butler said nothing for two years. Then Pharaoh had a couple of dreams that bothered him and couldn't find anybody who could tell him what they meant. One was about fat cows and skinny cows, and the other was similar, but about corn.

That's when the butler told Pharaoh about Joseph, and Pharaoh called for him. He told Joseph about his dreams, and Joseph told him they both meant the same thing—famine was coming. He was very specific: He said there would be seven years of prosperity, followed by seven years of famine. But he also told Pharaoh how to avoid the problem and have plenty while others were hungry. He told Pharaoh he should put aside a fifth of his harvest every year to tide him over during the famine.

> *When life strips you, God will always dress you. He knows your size.*

Pharaoh was so pleased that he put Joseph to work in the palace, heading up the collection effort. And, Genesis 41 tells us Pharaoh also gave Joseph four fine and very important gifts—a robe, a ring, a necklace, and a second chariot.

The robe replaced the one Joseph had lost when his brothers stripped him. That shows us that when life strips you, the king will always dress you. When life strips you, God will always dress you. He knows your size.

The ring represents authority since it carried the signet of the Pharaoh. He would put the signet of the ring on the documents so that everyone would know they were official.

The necklace represented the favor of the king. It gave access to those who wore it. So it meant Joseph was pretty important.

And, of course, the second chariot means protection. The first chariot went into battle. The second chariot followed. It never went first. And in life we sometimes get slapped around like cheap piñatas because we want to ride in the first chariot. We need to always let God ride in the first. We should ride in the second. That's our First Place—right behind God; following, with Him in the lead.

So Joseph's life story turned out pretty well, and his first dream became a reality: Because he worked for Pharaoh, and his brothers were ruled by Egypt, they did serve Joseph.

Joseph waited two years in prison after the butler got out, but look at what he got. He wanted out. He must have been wondering the whole time, "Why am I still here?" But that just shows us that God does things at the right time, not our time. Things don't always happen when you want them to; they happen when they're supposed to.

He served someone else's dream, and his dream became a reality. He handled the preparations for famine foretold in Pharaoh's dream and his brothers ended up serving him.

That's the power of a dream weaver:

Find someone else's dream that you can serve. Help someone else make their dream a reality. Your dream will never become a reality until you serve someone else's dream first.

> *Whatever we build in life, if it does not serve a greater cause, it will die.*

And it doesn't just happen in the Bible. We see it all around us.

Look at Bill Gates. For thirteen years in a row, until just before he stepped down as head of Microsoft in 2008, Bill Gates was the richest man on the planet.

His success story is well known: an incredibly bright computer geek writes the operating system that revolutionizes personal computing. Then he proves that he's even smarter than people realized by "licensing" the rights to other companies instead of just selling the program to them. He showed that he wasn't just a computer whiz, he also had tremendous business acumen.

Over the years that followed, Windows became the most widely used computer software in the world, and he made so much money that someone once calculated that he made about $1 million an hour over the years he was at Microsoft—so fast that if he dropped a $1,000 bill, he would *lose* money if he took the time to stop and pick it up; he'd make more money continuing with his work.

So how did he get rich? Great idea. Yes. Hard work. Yes. Brilliant business acumen. Yes. Absolutely.

But do you really think the teenaged Bill Gates who started tinkering with computers and tediously writing line after line of software code while he was still in middle school did it because he was thinking of getting rich?

Maybe. But even if he did, that wouldn't be enough. No. Not at all. Lots of kids have gone into computing, just like lots of kids have gone into acting and the law and medicine, and they haven't gotten rich—because they did it for the wrong reason. They did it to serve themselves.

Bill Gates fell in love with computing, and what it could do—for others, for the greater good. He may not have been thinking of it in those terms, especially not as a kid in school in Seattle, but his success came because what he created served a greater cause.

> *You can't succeed in life without some business acumen, and you can't succeed in business without Kingdom acumen.*

Business is an extension of the spiritual world. Many of the principles incorporated within a viable and successful business structure today are just Biblical Principles 101. Stewardship and due diligence, accountability and transparency, social responsibility and ethics—all of that is just what I refer to as "Wall Street Cathedral."

And vice versa. Business rules apply to the spiritual world, as well. The kingdom of God is a business. I am in my Father's business and in the business of the Kingdom.

So you can't really succeed in life, you can't form viable relationships and Kingdom partnerships, without having some sort of business acumen. And I don't mean having to go to business school at Wharton and get your MBA. I mean there must be some sort of notion of business sense, of responsible management and obligation and transparency and good governance.

You can't succeed in life without some business acumen, and you can't succeed in business without Kingdom acumen.

Bill Gates is a perfect example.

From the very beginning, people paid him because he gave them something that served *their* needs. His real dream—the true dream connected to his true Kingdom Culture purpose, whether he realized it or not—was to change the way we do things, to change the way we handle information, to change what we do with computers and what computers can do for us. And he succeeded so well that he not only changed what we do with computers, he changed the way we live. He revolutionized computing, and changed the world!

His dream became a reality because it served a greater cause. That's why Bill Gates grew to be the richest man on Earth.

Principle Four

There's Always an Empty Tomb
Right Before a Filled Upper Room

Chapter 33

SEASONS OF PREPARATION

There is always a season of preparation before the season of revelation. In our lives we have experiences, moments, people, and prayers that prepare the way. There is no such thing as immediate gratification or immediate satisfaction. There is always preparation. And faith is what prepares the way for fear. Faith gets there first to prepare the way for fear.

If faith made it and survived, fear says: "I have nothing left to fear." If John would have arrived first and come out and said, "I was wrong," would Peter still have gone in?

I doubt it. He needed John to prepare the way. He needed John to go ahead of him, to look in the tomb and to let him know that it was okay to go in. And that's what John did.

We have the same in our lives. We have people, and relationships, and prayers that have made sure the way is prepared for us. We have moments that have triggered the chain of events that have activated our futures, long before we arrive.

> *We were healed before we ever got sick. We were forgiven before we ever sinned. We were restored before we ever fell.*

It's not up to us. We don't have to send faith out first. From a Kingdom Principles perspective, God already did that. Faith already got there first for us.

God is a very proactive God. It's not like God is reacting to our silliness. He made the way before we even had the problems and the circumstances.

He made a way out before we were even imprisoned. He created the key for the cell before the cell and the iron and the steel were ever forged. He went to the cross so we wouldn't have to go to the cross. He paid the price so we wouldn't have to pay the price. He already ran and got there first.

So we don't have to. It doesn't require us to have a dichotomous moment. It doesn't require us to run, faith first, and touch the tomb and come back and then send fear. Faith already ran. That's great news: Faith already ran, got there and prepared the way.

If we understand that, it will change our outlook. As we resume our journey every day we can head out with the confidence that faith always gets there first. And it already did. We were healed before we ever got sick. We were forgiven before we ever sinned. We were restored before we ever fell. The Bible says, "the blood of Jesus cleanses us from all sin."[1] All sin. Not just past sin, but future sin as well.

Now it's our turn. Our faith is there. We're just catching up to it right now. If we activate it, all we have to do is just confront the fear and, every single day, die to live.[2]

That's having the faith *of* God in us. The fact that we know it's already done. What we have to do is accept that, embrace that, and allow that knowledge to lift us and carry us to our destiny.

---

1   1 John 1:7.
2   Galatians 2:20.

Chapter 34

THE PROMISE OF THE EMPTY TOMB

Mary Magdalene, Peter, and John ran toward the empty tomb and they found absolutely nothing. Right after that, God ran and gave them exactly what they needed, and more. God rewarded them. But He gave them a double portion.

And He didn't just do it for them. He does it for all of us. There is always a season when we run and find nothing, but that's only because God is about to run and give us everything—exceedingly, abundantly, and above all. There's always going to be an empty tomb right before a filled upper room.

There's always a desert before a promised land. There's always a wilderness experience before the execution of ministry, as with Christ.[1] There's always that dark moment before the sun rises.

> *There is a season that we run and find nothing,*
> *but that's only because God is about to run and give us everything—*
> *exceedingly, abundantly, and above all.*

The same thing applies to that person who had a bad relationship, who had a bad divorce. They go out and they find somebody else and it's going along fine and then they're disappointed again. Or the person who thought that this time they had worked hard enough and they were going to get that promotion, and they're disappointed.

They ran, they gave it everything, and in their vision at this moment, they found nothing.

---

1   Luke 4:1–13.

These are not the mediocre, halfhearted quitters. These are people who have given it their all, who have dotted every i, crossed every t, exerted energy beyond belief—even exceedingly, abundantly, above all they ever had. These are the ones who never gave up. They ran the race, completed the race, and at the end of the race found no reward.

If you find yourself in this situation, in that season, hold on. It only means one thing: God is about to run and give you everything.

Because here's what could have happened: They could've run into that empty tomb and found nothing, given up and turned away from Christ and his teachings. And they could've said, "That's it for me. It's over. It's finished. I quit. I'm never going to run again."

But they didn't. They ran. They found nothing. And they ran back to tell others what they had found.

God rewards those who run and find nothing, yet continue to believe that there must be something. Even if they have to run again, even if they have to run toward another tomb, they know—not think, suspect, or have a feeling, but really, truly *know*—that there's something great waiting for them.

> *There is always an empty tomb right before a filled upper room.*

We have it all wrong with respect to our lives. We have this idea that once we get the Wow! Factor, when we get the "It," the blessing, the glory—however we want to phrase it—we think that whenever we get that successful moment, when the dream is fulfilled or we accomplish our purpose, that that's when we have to be very careful, because things occur in our lives to try to steal it.

It's the other way around. It's totally the other way around.

What we have to be careful about is missing out on them in the first place. The rewards are there, waiting for us to find them. Once we get them, if they're truly the reward we're meant to have, then they can't be taken away. The way they get stolen is by us losing our way. Or by us rushing through the process, trying to skip steps, or take shortcuts. The rewards that are meant to be ours will always be ours. But only when they are meant to be.

Remember Joseph, with his multicolored robe? Joseph spent two extra years in prison waiting for the butler to mention his name to Pharaoh. Joseph did the butler a huge favor: he interpreted his dream and eased his mind, and, in the process, proved that nobody but nobody could interpret a dream like Joseph. And then what? He had to wait two more years before the butler told Pharaoh so Pharaoh would let Joseph out of jail. Two more years!

That's terrible. Or so it seems.

Joseph had his expectations. He put his hope in the butler. He ran for that dream—the butler will get me out of prison. And nothing. He ran and found nothing.

But wait a minute. Let's look at it a different way. What would have happened if the butler had been able to get Joseph out of prison right then? What would have happened if Joseph's dream had come true, if he had gotten something instead of finding nothing?

He probably would have just packed up and left. He would have said, "Okay, great. I'm out of prison, time to move on." He would have gotten out of prison, but he would have missed out on the big prize.

Instead, he found nothing when he first asked for it. And, two years later, God gave him heaping double portions, triple portions—exceedingly, abundantly, above all portions. Joseph got nothing. Then God gave him everything. God gave him more than he asked for, more than he ever expected.

If you feel that you are in prison, waiting for your release, and you try, and you try, and you try—and nothing! Hold on. That means it's coming—your reward, your release, your daybreak—whatever "It" is, is coming in ways far, far beyond your expectations.

If you have run your course, dotted your i's, crossed your t's, and found nothing, I want you to know that the very next thing that's about to happen in your life is that God is about to run and give you everything. There is always an empty tomb right before a filled upper room.

You are assured of a filled upper room. Assured! For every empty tomb there is a filled upper room.

And there may be more than one. The first door offers rewards, but it's not the only door. Beyond that one, through that very room, lies the path to even more treasures.

Chapter 35

SELF-EMPTYING EVERY DAY

When Mary Magdalene, Peter, and John were running, they were on their way to discover the big surprise that the tomb was empty. But they were also pushing themselves, straining themselves and draining themselves. They were running toward emptiness, and making themselves empty as they ran.

Mary Magdalene, Peter, and John ran until they had nothing left. They ran until they literally exhausted everything they had. And when they got where they were going, what they were looking for was not there, but they found other things that were.

It looked empty. It seemed like it was empty. But what they considered and perceived to be nothing was actually everything. By that place being empty, by running toward empty and finding nothing, their hearts were filled. Their lives were filled. Their space was filled.

In life, we need to run toward empty, too. We have to run and try as hard as we can, exert ourselves as much as we can, to empty ourselves of the spiritual, emotional, and psychological impediments that hold us back.

We need to run until we are empty in order to be filled again. In order to be replenished. In order to be restored and renewed. In order to remove from our system the pains and the sufferings and the negative energy, all the things from the past—the failure, the disappointment, the denials, the betrayals, the discouragement, the anxiety, the fears, the confusion.

We need to run until all of these things are gone. Let's run until anxiety is gone. Let's run on the energy of fear, until the fear is gone. Let's run until it's exhausted. Be it confusion, trepidation, angst, whatever that fear may be, negative or positive. Let us empty ourselves so that we can be renewed.

We all have to go through a moment of renewal. We can't live on the same thrust for all of our lives. There must be continuous renewal. There must be a continuous influx of new joy.

> *We need to run until we are empty in order to be filled again.*

The Bible says, His mercies are new every morning.[1] But that's not just a gift from God each day; it is a daily commitment to be renewed. You are supposed to use the energy that God gives you every day until it's gone.

Before you go to bed that night, all of the energy, all of the acumen, all of the joy, use it up! It's not there for hibernation.

The old model was: Let's preserve and reserve as much as possible for a rainy day. I'm not talking about financially; I'm talking about intrinsically, spiritually, mystically. The new model, the Kingdom model, the Path of Miracles model is: Use it up, because it's renewed every single morning.

Once we have emptied ourselves, once we have allowed ourselves to remove the impediments, we can then open ourselves and discover, yes, it's empty, but in fact it's filled with everything and God is about to fill us with everything.

We must empty ourselves every single day. Every single day, we must have an empty tomb experience. Every single day we must wake up in the morning with a commitment, and secure in the fact that the good Lord has given us divine provision—not just providence, but provision—that will enable us to execute that day in fullness.

But—and this is a big but!—we have the responsibility to exhaust and to make sure we use up everything He gives us by the time we lay our head down on a pillow in the evening. Don't go to bed without using that love, that joy, that peace, that mercy, that understanding. Don't go to bed unless you've used it all. Don't rest until it has been engaged, activated, spread, and shared.

Then, in the morning, we should get out of bed and try to spread around and use up and run as much as we can with the good works that God wants us to accomplish. But just because you're trying to empty yourself and you're

---

1 Lamentations 3:22–23, English Standard Version.

trying to give it all doesn't mean that you can. You have to make a massive effort to try, and that effort has to be sincere. It has to be meaningful and it has to be deliberate.

Now if you can go to bed and your conscience is clear,[2] knowing that on that day you did everything possible to exhaust everything in your arsenal, to exhaust all of that positive energy, that love, that fellowship, and that joy, then you have succeeded in unlocking the exceedingly, abundantly, above all that God has waiting for you.

> *We must empty ourselves every single day.*

"Empty" is a paradox. When you say "empty," that means in and of itself the absence of things. It means that you exhausted it all. But the fact is that it comes from a bottomless well. That's the paradox. It seems like that's impossible, that things can't work that way. But when I find my connection with God, when I find the faith *of* God inside me and I connect to it, it's a bottomless fountain. It's a well that never empties.

The faith of God never empties, but the faith of God gives birth to the realities, to the arrows in the quiver, to the strength, to the guidepost, to the virtues, to the fruit. It gives us all these tools, and these tools must be used daily.

You have to make a sincere effort to spread it around as much as you can and to empty yourself of all the bad things while you're filling yourself up with all the good things.

It's continuous. And it's daily.

We need to both fill up and empty ourselves. And it's a continuous process.

It's not recycling. It's a filtering process, where we examine the things in our lives on a daily basis, continuously, and we empty ourselves of all the elements that will hinder and impede and obstruct the free flow of God in us and through us—the free flow of love, the free flow of God's kingdom.

I am an instrument. I am a means. I am a vessel. I am the system through which God touches the Earth.

2　Acts 23:1; Acts 24:16.

You and I are the extension of God's Kingdom. And if there are things in our lives and elements in our lives that impede—be it negative thoughts, be it sin, be it unrighteousness, be it hatred or unforgiveness—then they inhibit our connection *to* God and they limit what we receive *from* God.

What do I mean? I don't mean that God denies us His gifts. No. The rewards are already there. But it's up to us to discover them on our journey. And if our connection is weak, if our vision is cloudy, if our hearing is fuzzy, then we can't see where God wants us to go and we can't hear what God is saying.

If we can't clear away the impediments, we are blind men tapping our canes in the darkness, unable to find our way. We are unable to find our true path, and it's our own fault.

> *When I find the faith of God inside me and I connect to it, it's a bottomless fountain. It's a well that never empties.*

Chapter 36

THE FIVE PRIMARY IMPEDIMENTS

There are five primary impediments to the free flow of God that we have to empty ourselves of on a daily basis.

1. Unforgiveness. Unforgiveness acts as a dam to the free flow of God's righteous stream. The beauty of God and his blessings are held back by unforgiveness.

That lack of forgiveness, that unforgiveness, will leave you unrewarded, unfulfilled, uncompleted. As long as you are chained by unforgiveness, bound by your unwillingness to release your rancor, you remain a slave to your bitterness and resentment, and you will never live exceedingly, abundantly, above all. You will never fulfill God's perfect purpose through your life and reach your complete destiny.

I know there are many who will say: "But that's outrageous. I was abused as a child. Horrific things were inflicted on me. How dare you say that I have to forgive?"

You have to. You have to if you want to be free. You have to if you want to live exceedingly, abundantly, above all. You have to if you want to open the Path of Miracles and discover the rewards that God has waiting for you.

> *The power of forgiveness, the power of forgiving, goes hand in hand with the power of being forgiven.*

Forgiveness provides a double release. It releases that person, and it releases you.

A person or a situation can only be held captive by one thing: unforgiveness. If you are yet to forgive that father who abused you, you literally hold that person hostage to your unforgiveness. The destiny of that person, the reaping and sowing principle, mercy executed, it requires you to deliver them, to free them.

There is a mighty God who knows all things and who can judge them far better than we can. And that just God, that God who loves and who judges, can do it in a way that assures that it is done in perfect truth. It is perfect will.

My forgiveness releases that person to be judged by the Supreme Judge.

And it releases me from my past. The power of forgiveness, the power of forgiving, goes hand in hand with the power of being forgiven.

That is that incredible idea that Christ presented, which is: "forgive us our trespasses as we forgive those who trespass against us."[1]

To me, that is the most remarkable truth ever shared in the history of mankind. What power and audacity! What a grandiose notion! Complete forgiveness.

And Luke tells us that there's a very clear downside for not forgiving. He says Jesus was very specific about the ramifications of forgiveness and unforgiveness. He wrote that Christ said: "For if you forgive others for their transgressions, your heavenly father will also forgive you. But if you do not forgive others, then your father will not forgive your transgressions."[2]

So we have to empty ourselves of unforgiveness.

2. *The Micromanagement of Destiny*. We also have to free ourselves from what I call the micromanagement of destiny. Basically that means we don't need to know all the details.

To be honest, at times, the what, why, when, where, or how is not important. Not even the who is important—as long as we have enough faith in us to put our trust in God.

We have to free ourselves from having to know all the details. We have to free ourselves of the thought process that says: "Unless God puts everything out on the table, in some projected cosmic display, and describes to me the intricacies of His detailed plan and manifest destiny for my personal existence, I will not go any further."

That's ludicrous.

---

1   Matthew 6:12.
2   Matthew 6:14–15.

At times we desire to see specificity from God—we want the specifics, the detailing. "Show us the blueprint and we'll believe you."

But what we need to do is go into that well of faith, that never-ending fountain and supply of faith, and know that we do not have to fill in all the blanks.

We have to empty ourselves of the need of knowing every detail and leave it to God. He's a power bigger than us who knows all the details.

> *We have to empty ourselves of the need of knowing every detail and leave it to God.*

God's got it. I don't have to worry about that. He made the plan, and it unfolds exactly the way he intended.

Why should I worry?

We're heading down the highway He laid out for us. Why do I have to know every tiny detail?

I don't worry about every nut and bolt and wire in my car as I drive down the road in the everyday, physical world. I don't worry about how much paint was used or how much time it took or how many workers were needed to paint the lanes on the road. I don't get hung up about how the highway signs were made, or where, or by whom. I just read the signs to tell me where I'm going, I follow the road toward my destination, and I let the car do what it's supposed to do.

If I don't worry about every little rock in the road, or every stitch in my car seats—if I don't worry about these things made by people right here— why should I worry about every tiny detail of God's grand plan?

I don't need to worry about every raindrop. I can just leave it to God.

I only worry because I doubt. I don't trust the pilot, so I insist on knowing everything about the plane and the flight path. But God knows where we're going, and He knows how to get us there.

We've seen those bumper stickers that say, "Jesus is my copilot." I would argue that they have it wrong. The truth is, God is the pilot and Christ is the navigator who shows us the way, but I'm the copilot. I get to take the controls for most of the flight. God helps me take off, and if I get into trouble, He's there to help me steady my wings and get back on course. But I'm the one who's doing the flying. Hence the other bumper sticker: "If God is your CO-Pilot . . . SWITCH SEATS!"

3. Auto-dependency. In our twenty-first-century, individualistic, superhyper, intrinsically coerced reality, we believe we have the power to accomplish all things. But that is a notion we have to empty ourselves of—auto-dependency, self-dependency.

There is a higher power. There is a power beyond us, above us and around us, that knows more than we do and can do more than we can, in every way imaginable.

We have to go back to the point of acknowledging, of our believing in that power, and of submitting ourselves to that power.

> *We need to recognize and accept God's glory.*

That's a controversial concept. The word "submission" is a controversial term in our twenty-first-century world. But I don't mean submission in the sense of surrendering our free will. God doesn't want that. God gave us free will for a reason. He doesn't want blind followers. He wants the faithful with their eyes wide open, who see the wonder and splendor of what He gives us and believe because of what they see, not because of what they don't. I mean submission in the sense of yielding, which comes freely from within us because we recognize and accept God's glory.

Yes, there are things in this world that we need to do. Yes, we have the Spiritual DNA inside of us. But it comes from God. It's not a self-created DNA. The Good Lord, in that spiritual genome, in that Kingdom Culture DNA, deposited in us the ingredients for our success.

We activate it. We turn it on. But there are times when our own strength will not be sufficient. We need to believe that the partner we spoke about, my first senior collaborator, my first senior partner, is God. And with God all things are possible.

4. Fear. The daily emptying of fear is vital. The daily crucifixion of fear is vital.

We talked about the positive and negative power of fear earlier in this book.

We can run next to it. We can even use it as a guidepost. However, we cannot let it capture us. We cannot let it hold us hostage.

Fear is productive and can serve as a motivator and as a positive energy source only if it's on the outside. But intrinsically it's counterproductive. We know that it's counterproductive because it's the opposite of faith.

Faith and fear cannot occupy the same space. The fact that faith can run next to fear and faith is up to the challenge, as we saw with Peter and John, is amazing. We know who gets there first, and we know what happens. But faith and fear cannot occupy the same space. Fear has its own domain and faith has its. Faith is the enemy of fear. Faith is the antithesis of fear. Faith seeks, while fear hides. And faith sees everything fear does not.

So, while we have fear we can't open ourselves up to faith—not completely. Side by side is one thing. But they can't be in the same lane and they can't be occupying the same space. Because our inner being, our Spirit Person, is a domain of faith. It was created for faith. It was designed for faith. And whenever our spirit and our Soul Person, whenever our spiritual being, is not in perfect alignment with what it was created for, we cannot succeed.

Fear is an obvious impediment because fear prevents us from doing things. Fear of my past relationships, of repeating that bad experience, prevents me from going on and opening myself to new experiences. Fear of losing my job prevents me from doing the best job I possibly can because I'm afraid to stand up and be noticed. I don't want to stand up in the crowd.

Fear is such a primary, fundamental impediment. Living in fear is a terrible thing. It prevents so much. It keeps us from love. It keeps us from living. From feeling. From reaching our potential.

That's fear. It very well may be the primary obstacle to exceedingly, abundantly, above all.

> *While we have fear we can't open ourselves up to faith.*

That's why every single day we have to run toward empty. We have to make sure every single day that we confront our fears, so we reveal faith, we activate faith in fullness, and we saturate our lives and our communities and our surroundings with that faith.

5. *Anxiety*. Anxiety seems like an odd term to think of as an impediment. But think of all the Xanax and Valium recipients of the world. Why do they exist? Why do so many people have to take drugs to calm them? There are those who are truly mentally ill and need those drugs, of course. I'm not talking about them. I'm talking about those who feel the need to escape the pressures of the world we live in.

It's because we lead such a hurried and cumbersome existence.

Think about it: every day, all day, most of us are assailed and assaulted by duties and responsibilities, details and distractions, interruptions and interferences. All day, every day.

Worse yet, floating over all of it, permeating all of it: worries. Even when we've caught up with our work and we finally have the time to relax, we worry about paying our bills, about the health of our loved ones, about the floodwater rising on the river by town, about tornadoes and wildfires. We worry about whether there will be layoffs at the company we work for, about whether we'll get that raise or that promotion we're hoping for. We worry about all the things we wish would come, and about all the things we hope won't.

It's an amazing thing—once we know that we have the faith of God, once we activate all the principles previously mentioned, once we identify ourselves in our Kingdom DNA, then we know destiny is before us. We know that exceedingly, abundantly, above all is not some unreachable goal. It is assured based on faith.

Once we have all of that, the enemy that arises, and the one we have to deal with, is anxiety. Anxiety: When will it happen? Can it happen quicker? Can we accelerate the process? We have the anxiety of not knowing.

Anxiety develops and anxiety exposes its ugly head when we do not have all the facts. When we are lacking information that we find vital. Anxiety is the cousin of insecurity. It arises when we are not 100 percent secure. Anxiety is the by-product of vulnerability. If you are not vulnerable, then why would you be anxious? Anxiety speaks to our vulnerabilities, to our shortcomings, to our fear.

But the Bible tells us not to be anxious. It says, in no uncertain terms:

"Be anxious for nothing, but everything through prayer, supplication and thanksgiving. Let your requests be made known unto God."[3]

That's powerful. It acknowledges the fact that anxiety is one of those primary impediments.

Anxiety has the capability of facilitating a path toward insanity. We know that medically. We know that psychologically. We know that neurologically. That's truth. Many mental illnesses stem from the core base of Tier 1 anxieties. If Tier 1 anxiety is not dealt with appropriately, both medically and therapeutically, it can lead to a myriad of medical and mental issues.

Wherever fear is, that anxiety is not too far away. It is very unusual for fear to walk alone without anxiety somewhere nearby. I'm anxious because I'm fearful. And, at times, you're fearful because you're anxious.

Now, in my world—theologically, spiritually—I see anxiety not only as a medical condition that can be physiologically induced or traumatically induced. I see it as a spirit: the spirit of anxiety. Because anxiety arises from the activation of that Flesh Person to its fullest, without the full activation of the Spirit Person.

Be anxious for nothing. Let your requests be known to God.

Anxiety speaks to doubt; and doubt, of course, to unbelief. It joins the incredible team that lines up to oppose faith: fear, anxiety, doubt, and unbelief—they speak to the opposite of faith. Anxiety speaks to the opposite of security, assurance, perseverance, hope.

Therefore, you must rid yourself of anxiety. You must empty yourself of that anxiousness.

And you do that by first affirming the fact that there is a God who literally has stated to His people: "Speak to me."

There, the five primary impediments—unforgiveness, the micromanagement of destiny, auto-dependency, fear, and anxiety. Free yourself of those and you open yourself to the free flow of God in your life. Free yourself of those and you remove the obstacles you place in your own path. Free yourself of those, and you open the way to the Path of Miracles.

---

3   Philippians 4:6.

Chapter 37

PRAYER, SUPPLICATION, AND THANKSGIVING

You must have daily communication with someone higher than yourself, daily communication with the Almighty, daily communication with God. That's how you rid yourself of anxiety.

The Bible says it: "Prayer, supplication, and thanksgiving."[1]

There it is. It's simple. God asked us for three things.

First, He asked us for prayer. He told us to talk to Him. That means every day. He wants to hear from us. That doesn't mean you have to get on your knees and go through a litany of prayers, or recite the Lord's Prayer a hundred times. It doesn't have to take an hour. It can be a minute. A simple "hello" is all it takes, to let God know that you're thinking about Him. That's the important part—letting God know He's in your thoughts. Because He knows that if He's in your thoughts, He's in your heart. And that's what counts.

Second, supplication. He said, "Whatever you have in your heart regardless of how hurtful it may be or how painful or how severe and serious and pertinent it may be, go ahead and tell me." That's supplication.

And third, thanksgiving. He asked us to give thanks, but not just for the things we have. He wants us to give thanks for the things we have yet to receive. He wants you to celebrate the things you have yet to acquire. Thank Him for the things you do not see. Give thanks for the things that are not even in your hands yet. Give thanks for the things that you haven't experienced yet.

I'll put it another way you may be more familiar with: Count your blessings.

---

1   Philippians 4:6.

But not just count the blessings you know—not just for your wonderful spouse and your beautiful children and your mother and father; not for that lovely flower, that beautiful sunrise, or the butterfly that landed on your porch; and not for that great dinner, or the promotion you got at work, or the tax refund arriving early.

Count those, but not *just* those. Count your blessings, and give thanks for the ones you *haven't* received yet.

That's the awesomeness of that Scripture. It's prophetic. It's foresight. It's not about now. It's full acknowledgment of the notion that, "Yes, I may yet have to receive it, but I know it's mine. I know it's coming." It's a type of ownership.

I can give thanks because I *know* it's on the way. It's guaranteed. It's assured.

You know the adage: If life gives you lemons, make lemonade. If it gives you rocks, build an altar. Whatever it may be. If life gives you a storm and you fall off the ship, go swimming. If life puts you in the furnace, get a tan and come out shining.

> *Count your blessings, and give thanks for the ones you* haven't *received yet.*

God has already told me to rid myself of anxiety, to empty myself of it every day, and, best of all, He already told me how.

He gave me a spiritual recipe to rid myself of anxiety: prayer, supplication, and thanksgiving. It's the antidote to anxiety. He gave me that formula so that I can empty myself of anxiety, and He said, "Be still and know that I am God."[2]

That's God telling us: "Relax, it's going to be all right." That's what He's saying. It's "peace, be still."

It's what Christ said to the disciples when they were crossing the lake in a boat and the storm came upon them while he was sleeping.[3] They got nervous. They became anxious. And when the water started coming in,

---

2   Psalm 46:10, New International Version.
3   Mark 4:35–42.

they woke him up and asked him to do something because they were afraid they were going to sink. Christ turned to the storm and said, "Please, BE STILL!" and it calmed down.

Then he turned back to the disciples. And what does Christ say to them? "You didn't have to wake me up. I told you not to wake me up. You could have done this yourselves. Ye of little faith. You have the ability. It's within you."

Well, that's what God says to us: the kingdom of God is within you.[4] You have the ability.

The purpose of God was for the apostles, in the midst of the storm, to thrive. Not to be anxious. For them to change in the midst of the storm and not permit the storm to change them.

How can Christ be resting in the midst of the storm? Because it is the rest periods of our lives that enable us to wake up and confront the storms that come our way and guarantee success.

Don't be anxious. Do the opposite. When the storm comes, take a nap. Depend on God. Rest. Don't develop the fourteen steps for dealing with it, the twelve-step plan for confronting it—that time will come later.

Here's the one step: Be still and know that God is God.

Be still and know that God is God.

---

4   Luke 17:21, New International Version.

Chapter 38

THE WITHERING POWER OF DOUBT

We have to have faith that God knows what he is doing. We have to believe that our rewards are coming. We have to believe in Him. And we have to believe in ourselves.

When we doubt, we undermine ourselves. Doubt weakens us. Doubt is what stops us from making the leap we need to succeed. The gap between us and our goal seems like a giant gaping canyon, instead of a crack in the sidewalk that we can easily step over. Doubt makes every hill seem like an insurmountable mountain.

And doubt feeds our fear. Because it makes our enemies seem like giants and our obstacles appear immense, it intensifies our fears. Instead of seeing a river we have to cross, we see an ocean. And because we doubt our abilities, because we don't have faith that God is there by our side, we see ourselves drowning instead of swimming easily across.

When we empty ourselves of doubt, we cut our enemies down to size. We lose that magnifying lens that makes our obstacles seem huge. We see things for what they are.

Emptying ourselves of doubt fills us with confidence—*realistic* confidence, not overconfidence. Ridding myself of doubt doesn't make me suddenly believe I can fly. I can't jump off of tall buildings and land unhurt. No! Emptying myself of doubt lets me see the truth. It lets me see reality. I won't think an anthill is a skyscraper blocking my way. And I won't think I can leap tall buildings in a single bound.

> *Doubt stops us from making the leap we need to succeed.*

There are three levels of doubt.

The first is doubting God, doubting that He is there when you need Him, doubting as the disciples did that we are going to be safe in the storm.

The second is doubting yourself.

And the third is doubting what I call the community or the Kingdom.

The first one of course is self-explanatory. Doubting God is the primary error that so many of us make. It really and truly impedes so many of the blessings and the breakthroughs and the positive outcomes destined for us.

Doubting ourselves is equally important. We doubt ourselves constantly: Do I really have the acumen? Do I really have the wherewithal and the fortitude to accomplish this goal? To build this dream? Do I have it? And if I don't have it, can I get it somewhere? Is there a source where I can get it? Do I have the resources, and if not, can I find the resources?

There's a huge difference between recognizing where you need to partner and in doubting your ability to go forward. There's a huge difference between recognizing your limitations and doubting yourself. There's a difference between doing our due diligence and being truthful and transparent in exposing what our shortcomings may be in order to address them accordingly.

Our problem is that we doubt the purpose. We doubt the objective. And that's where the rubber hits the road. It's what Peter felt as he walked on water. It is those moments when we take our eyes off the prize. It is those moments in life when we really run toward empty that the doubt looms large and we wonder if we really have what it takes to make it.

You overcome that doubt by knowing that God trusts you and believes in you. God believes in you. After you believe in God, understand that it's reciprocated. At times, He believes in us even before we believe in Him. And God believes in us even when we don't believe in ourselves. He believes that I have within me what I need in order to do His will.

> *God believes in us even when we don't believe in ourselves.*

Doubting God, doubting self, and doubting those that God has placed around me fosters a culture of doubt. When we begin to surround ourselves with people and we do not believe in their abilities and their skills—in their calling, in their purpose, in their passion, in their promise, or in their King-dom DNA—then we create and foster a culture of doubt.

In my Life Surrounded, I want to make sure that those closest to me are faith, commitment, and honor, rather than betrayal, doubt, and denial. I want to surround myself with goodness and mercy and signs and wonder. I want to surround myself with dream weavers and not dream killers.

And, every day, I want to run toward empty.

I begin by confronting my doubts. The first thing I do every morning, the instant I open my eyes, is say: It's confrontation time! Every morning!

I ask myself: What are the things that I need to confront in order to bring about revelation, to bring about activation, to bring about saturation? What's my challenge today? What's my goal? What's my mission statement? What's my purpose? This very day! What are the things I need to over-come?

And I make this affirmation, every morning:

I will not doubt. As our Lord told us, "Fear not!"[1]

I may not have all the resources, but I have a source. There is a fountain. There is an everlasting, never-ending fountain where I can obtain the tools and the ingredients necessary for success. I know that if I fall short, there is One who will lead me all the way.

God is with me. I will not doubt.

---

1   Isaiah 35:4; John 12:15.

Chapter 39

THE FIERY FURNACE

Yₒu've probably heard the story of Shadrach, Meshach, and Abednego, or read it in the Bible.[1]

King Nebuchadnezzar ordered these three young Hebrew men to bow down before him and to worship a golden idol. When they refused, he ordered them thrown into a furnace.

The Bible describes it as a "fiery furnace," and it says that before the king had the three thrown in he actually ordered the guards to feed the fire and increase the heat. Seven times they increased the fire.

Then Shadrach, Meshach, and Abednego were placed in chains and they were thrown into the fire. The flames were so hot that even the Babylonian guards who threw them in were burned and died immediately because of the intensity of the fire.

But, the Bible says, when the king looked in through a window in the door, he didn't see them burning. Rather, he saw a fourth man—a fourth man!—standing in the flames with them. The king said the man looked like the Son of God. He had radiant golden hair. And he was standing there in the flames with Shadrach, Meshach, and Abednego—and none of the four was burning.

The Bible never says that Shadrach, Meshach, and Abednego ever saw that man in the fire. Never.

And that proves the point: It really doesn't matter if you see God in the midst of the hell you're going through. What matters is that your enemies see God in the midst of the hell you're going through.

---

1 Daniel 3:8–30, English Standard Version.

> *It really doesn't matter if you see God in the midst of the hell you're going through. What matters is that your enemies see Him.*

There are opposing forces in our lives, spiritual or otherwise, which will surrender the moment they see God in the midst of your fire. So this notion that if I run and I don't see God, in this very moment, in this very place where I need Him and I thought I would find Him and I don't see Him—the idea that that somehow means God has abandoned me is wrong.

We need to change that and say, "God, I would prefer to see you, but it's all right if I don't as long as my enemy, as my circumstances, as my doubts and my fear and my confusion and these things that have risen against me—as long as these opposing forces from Hell or Earth see you, then I'm fine."

God is there, even when we don't see Him.

John and Peter ran, and when they looked in they saw nothing. They did not find what they were looking for. All they found was folded linen.

There are going to be times in our lives when we go and we expect, and we try and we search, and when we find nothing we are going to say, "God, why did you abandon me? You weren't there."

If He's not there when you get there, it's not that He abandoned you. Not at all. If He's not there when you get there it only means that He is actually fighting the battle for you. If you don't see Him in front of you, it's because He's behind you.

In the book of Exodus the Bible says that God turned around and became the rear guard of the people of Israel as they marched out to cross the Red Sea.[2] He was fighting the battle. He became the rear guard.

The Bible says He was a cloud by day and a fire by night. It says He was in front of them, in a cloud, a pillar of smoke, leading them. When night came, he became a fire, to lead them with its light.

> *If you don't see God in front of you, it's because He's behind you.*

---

2 Exodus 14:19.

But then, when the enemy got near, God literally turned away from them and went behind them to defend them. He became the rear guard.

When we don't see God in front of us, it only means that He is fighting the battle behind us. He's actually fighting the battle for us. He has promised never to leave us or abandon us. He's always with us. Whether we see Him or not.

Chapter 40

FINDING THE UNEXPECTED

You will always have a season when you will run and pursue your dream and find nothing. You will run and you will literally find nothing first. Then you will discover that that nothing is actually everything.

There comes a season when you run in the dark, when you select a partner, when you have all of the affirmations that we mentioned in previous chapters, and when you arrive, there is nothing. Actually, it appears empty, it *appears* void, but it's actually full of something.

That emptiness exposes what you are really looking for. In other words, what you thought you were looking for may not necessarily have been what you were really looking for, or what you needed. And, in His divine wisdom, God provides this opportunity where you run and you do not necessarily find what you expect—you find what you need.

It's not what you were looking for, but it's what you need. That empty tomb speaks prophetically about finding the unexpected. It speaks about life's great surprises. It's not necessarily finding what I wanted—finding my dream, finding my perfect day, finding my perfect moment—but what God knows I really need.

That's often a great surprise. We think we know what we're looking for. We think we know what we need. But God knows better.

> *What you thought you were looking for may not necessarily have been what you were really looking for, or what you needed.*

The late Michael Crichton, the author of *Jurassic Park*, *The Terminal Man*, and more than a dozen other novels, went to medical school before he began writing. His books have enriched, entertained, and enlightened millions. But he thought he was going to be a doctor. He started writing under a pseudonym, using a pen name, to support himself while he studied. Then came *Andromeda Strain*, while he was doing postdoctoral work at the Salk Institute, and he discovered that what he had been looking for—a career in medicine—was not what he needed. It wasn't his purpose. God knew.

Something very similar happened to Sir Arthur Conan Doyle. The man who invented Sherlock Holmes and showed the world how deductive reasoning, detailed observation, and logic could solve crime also began writing as a medical student. In fact, he based the brilliant detective on one of his medical school professors, who taught his students that they had to look for all the signs and clues in a patient's symptoms to properly diagnose the disease. Doyle even went on two voyages as a ship's doctor, still looking for a career in medicine, before God gave him what he really needed, and his career as a writer took off.

And, a story we all know: Christopher Columbus. He was looking for a new route to India. He discovered a New World. A new route would have given Spain a competitive advantage in the marketplace, a way to deliver the much-desired spices from India faster. That, in turn, would have earned Columbus a reputation as a great captain and explorer, which pretty much would have guaranteed him financial success and comfort. But what Columbus went looking for is not what he found. God knew what he needed, and he gave it to him in portions Columbus could have never imagined.

I remember, when I was about fourteen years old, a terrible storm hit Pennsylvania and the river next to our apartment complex overflowed and we were flooded. I don't mean we had some water damage to the rug. I mean that, literally, we had four and a half feet of water coming into the apartment. My dad had to rescue our neighbor. It was only four and a half feet, but at that moment she saw her furniture floating and she couldn't swim and she panicked. He had to go in and carry her out.

We lost everything. The furniture. The television. The bed. Clothes. Pictures. I had my baseball card collection with a Mickey Mantle and a Yogi Berra, and my Reggie Jackson '77 card. And it was gone. Everything was gone.

My dad had been laid off from work and the union pay he got was gone just paying for a hotel. We had zero. I remember seeing him with this look on his face that seemed to say, "Oh, God. Where do we go from here?"

That was the first time I questioned God. I asked Him, "Why? Couldn't you have stopped this?"

Well, I didn't realize it right away, but the answer was, "Yes. Of course. But, you'll see, I did it on purpose. And you'll thank me for it."

And, you know what? He was right.

What I saw was this: I saw my mom and dad get closer together than ever before. I saw us as a family unit come together cohesively like never before. I experienced joy.

My parents turned that flood experience into a moment of rebuilding, repurchasing everything from new furniture to a new car. Instead of the end, it was a new beginning. It was more of a, "Watch, out of this chaos, out of this disorder will come order and it will be better than before."

I always had some sort of biblical narrative that substantiated me in my most difficult times of life. This one was the story of Jacob and the ladder.[1] That he put his head on a rock and he saw a ladder.

What I heard from God after that flood was that for every rock there must be a ladder, and for every hard place there must be a dream. The most difficult of places facilitates the greatest of dreams and blessings and break-throughs.

That's what I heard from God. And I understood that. It was totally unexpected. We didn't find what we were looking for, but we found something much greater. We found what we needed.

So did Peter, John, and Mary Magdalene. None of them found what they were looking for. Not a single one of them found what he or she was looking for. They all found something much, much, *much* more valuable.

Does that sound like exceedingly, abundantly, above all? Does that sound like God delivering more than you ever asked for, more than you ever expected? It should, because it is. That's the way God does it.

They went looking for Christ's body. They went looking for death. And they found life eternal. They found resurrection and the promise of everlasting life in paradise.

If that's not exceedingly, abundantly, above all, I don't know what is.

---

1 Genesis 28:11-19.

And it didn't just stop with them. He gave us all the promise of everlasting life. Every single one of us. He gave us all the promise of exceedingly, abundantly, above all.

We just have to recognize it.

> *You do not necessarily find what you expect—you find what you need.*

Sometimes—no, oftentimes—we have blinders on. We're looking for something and that's all we're willing to see. It's that old joke about the minister in the flood, who kept saying, "God will deliver me."

The minister was the head of a church in a town where the river started to flood and everyone was told to evacuate. A car came by, and the people inside offered the minister a ride and he said, "No. You go ahead. God will deliver me." The car drove off and the water kept rising. The minister had to climb up on the church's roof to stay dry. He looked up to the sky and prayed, and a boat came by. The people inside offered him a ride, but the minister said, "No. You go ahead. God will deliver me." So the boat went on and the water kept rising and the minister had to climb all the way up to the top of the steeple to stay dry. He kept praying, and a helicopter came by, and the pilot offered him a ride. But the minister waved him away. He said, "No. You go ahead. God will deliver me."

And he drowned. And when he got to heaven, he sees God and asks, "What happened? I thought you were going to deliver me?"

And God says, "What do you think the car, the boat, and the helicopter were for?"

The minister was so busy looking for God to deliver him he couldn't see the ways God was trying to.

> *The empty tomb speaks not to what was, but to what will be.*

Mary Magdalene, Peter, and John all ran to that tomb expecting to find one thing and, instead, they found in that empty place what they needed to continue in their lives and to have success in their future.

So there are moments in life when we exert an incredible amount of energy, where we run and pursue and do the right things and make the right affirmations, establish the right relationships, adopt the right culture, engage and activate the right DNA, the Kingdom DNA—and we still run and find nothing.

That season of finding nothing is not a negative thing.

Embedded within that emptiness is where we find the core nuggets and threads that are necessary for success in the future. That empty tomb spoke to the future. That empty tomb—that nothingness, that state of nothing, of absolute void, the absence of the accomplished desire, the accomplished goal; after exerting energy, after spending money, after spending so much time and nurturing relationships—that emptiness speaks to what is coming.

That empty tomb speaks not to our wants but to our needs. The empty tomb speaks not to what was, but to what will be.

Mary Magdalene, Peter, and John ran and found nothing. Then God ran and filled them with everything they needed. Not just what they needed to survive. It was never a commitment for survival, but rather a commitment for success.

God never called any of His children to "just survive." He never called us to live "just enough" in any level. He called us for success—and He means within the complete description of success, Kingdom success, not just in man's interpretation of success. Not just in materialistic means and worldly gains, but, more important, in spiritual and emotional, relational, Kingdom ways.

That's why we are more than conquerors; we're more than just victors. Romans 8:37 speaks to the fact that He fought the battle, but we obtained the prize. Specifically, the Bible says, "We overwhelmingly conquer through Him who loved us."

Overwhelmingly!

PRINCIPLE FIVE

ORDER PRECEDES PROMOTION

Chapter 41

FOLDED LINEN

When Mary Magdalene stepped into the tomb she saw the mercy seat—the throne of God. According to Scripture, the mercy seat was the seat of atonement, which was sprinkled with sacrificial blood to cleanse the sins of humanity. The Bible tells us that God Himself described how it should be made, with two cherubim—two angels—facing each other from either end, with their wings stretched out to cover it.[1]

That's what Mary Magdalene saw: two angels sitting beside the slab where Christ's body had been placed.[2] Christ, whose blood had been spilled to take away the sins of the world.[3] The body was gone, but two angels sat at either end.

A few minutes later, Peter and John walked into the same place, but they didn't see angels. They saw folded linen.[4]

That's what's amazing about this. John 20 reveals that Mary Magdalene saw the mercy seat, and angels. Peter and John never saw two angels. Peter and John saw folded linen. Perfectly placed, as Scripture says. The head garb was there, and the rest of the linen folded and perfectly placed. Three people walk into the same place and see different things.

What does this tell us? It tells us that once we activate these Kingdom Principles and we reach that empty tomb, we will see different things. Someone else can walk into your journey and into your experience, into that circumstance, and take something out of it that is totally different from what you took out of it. Because what you take out of it is directly proportional to your personal narrative and journey.

---

1   Exodus 25:17–22.
2   John 20:12.
3   John 1:29.
4   John 20:4–7.

> *There is no way God will ever bless the next chapter, the next stage of our lives, until all the areas currently in our lives are in perfect order.*

Mary Magdalene saw the mercy seat. She saw two angels. One at the head part, one at the feet part.

Do you know what that speaks to? It speaks to the Old Testament, the Jewish Bible, the Ark of the Covenant. What Mary Magdalene saw was the glory of God in the tomb—the mercy seat, where forgiveness took place.

A woman who had experienced forgiveness saw forgiveness. She was empowered by visually engaging the personification and the embodiment of forgiveness—the mercy seat.

Nothing else personifies forgiveness to the Jewish people more than the mercy seat and the sacrificial exercise, the expiatory work, the Day of Atonement, the shedding of innocent blood. That's what the two angels Mary Magdalene saw represent—one at that head part and one at the feet. When Mary Magdalene stepped into the empty tomb, she saw the mercy seat.

But then Peter and John stepped in, and they saw folded linen. They saw order: Because order precedes promotion.

There is no way God will ever bless the next chapter, the next stage of our lives, until all the areas currently in our lives are in perfect order. We need to put order in our houses. Put order in our finances. Put order in our spiritual walk with God. Put order spiritually and emotionally, physically, financially, corporately, communally—we need to incorporate order.

Order precedes promotion.

> *The time to put things in order is when they're in disarray.*

We have to dot the i's and cross the t's of our relationships, of our careers, and of our lives before we can discover our rewards. We have to be meticulous and precise, fill in all the particulars, cover every detail, make sure everything is as it should be. We must have order in our lives before we can collect our rewards.

When? Now.

Do you wait for everything to be going great? No. Do you wait for your bank account to be full to pay off all your bills? No. Because your bank account will never be full if you let your bills build up.

The time to put things in order is when they're in disarray. When we're having trouble in our relationships. When the factory we've been working at for fifteen years is closing. When we're having a hard time making ends meet.

That's the perfect time to put things in order. The perfect time to put them in order is when we don't have enough. When we have to apply the faith gene and the faith of God.

That's the time to put things in order, not when we have exceedingly, abundantly, above all. It's not when we have our certificate of deposit and we have our investments and we have our stock portfolio and we have our financial prospectus. It's when we don't have. It's the opposite.

It's when we have nothing that we have everything. Because the Bible says that the last shall be first and the first shall be last.[5] The Bible says that the meek shall inherit the earth.[6]

My friend Daniel Delgado learned that when he saw the success he had built vanish, and had to start all over again.

Daniel worked his way up the ladder on Wall Street during the exuberant economic boom of the 1990s. By 1997, he had his own company and was busily investing in a number of ventures, using the same techniques he had learned in some of the nation's top financial firms. In business, they call it leveraging. In Las Vegas, they call it gambling—big!

He used borrowed money—from other people, lines of credit, and credit cards—hedging his bets with capital ventures that were profitable, for a time. Then came September 11, and it all crashed down.

His investments went sour. His profits disappeared. He spent his savings, refinanced his homes. Finally, he declared bankruptcy.

He was out of work, his credit ruined, financially insolvent. But he didn't just sit and watch his debt mount. Daniel realized he couldn't borrow his way out of debt. He identified needs from wants, and paid with cash for any need purchased. He and his family cut all unnecessary expenses, including cell

5   Matthew 20:16.
6   Matthew 5:5, New International Version.

phones and cable, they sold off one car, eliminated vacations, bagged lunch, and—most important—created a budget.

One thing they didn't cut, though, was their tithes. "What we implemented with the savings was to sow more into ministry," he says.

Then, after sixteen months, the miracles began. "When we increased our giving, financial doors started to open," he says. "We saw the little we had go further than ever before. Consulting opportunities opened that led to offers for full-time employment. I experienced favor as never before in my life."

He initiated a plan to repay his debt. And, three years after that first door opened, he took a position in an asset management firm making a six-figure salary with bonus and benefits.

The lesson: He had, and lost. He gave, and got. When he recognized and applied the Kingdom Principles in his life, he found himself back on the Path of Miracles.

Kingdom Principles are in many cases the opposite of how we see things in our materialistic, individualistic mind-set. Our earthly vision is not Kingdom reality. And if I want to see God's kingdom come then I must do the absurd. And the absurd is that when I don't have enough money to pay for gas, that's when I sit down with my family and say, "Let's put these weak finances in order."

Sit them down and take a hard look at your financial and economic reality.

Number one. Are we spending more than what we actually bring in?

Number two. Are there areas in our lives where we are financially irresponsible in respect to credit cards, in respect to erroneous investment?

Number three. Most important and above all things, are we giving to God, are we giving to charity? Are we financing God's kingdom and are we financing God's Kingdom Economy for my life? Are we financing God's good works—taking care of the poor, doing charitable work, helping those in need? Especially when I am in my greatest need. That's when I have to reach out and help somebody else.

> *Our earthly vision is not Kingdom reality.*

Putting order in your life is not just about finances. It's not just about balancing the books. It doesn't end when you can pay your bills. It extends to every part of your life, not just the financial. In fact, even if that's the area where I'm feeling and seeing the most obvious pain, that's not the area where I would begin.

I would look at my family. I would look at my relationships. I would begin not with the economy, but with my walk with God. With my walk *in* God.

What's lacking? Is it daily prayer? Meditation? Reflection? Are you taking time every day to count your blessings, to give proper thanks to the Lord?

That doesn't mean you have to go to a church service every day (though doing so would only help!). And it doesn't mean you have to set aside an hour or two on your knees every day. But you should take a few minutes to reflect, to be still. A single heartfelt thank-you—one that really, truly comes from the heart; not because you have to, or to get it out of the way, but because you honestly feel it and want to—is worth ten thousand forced prayers.

Is there order in my physical being? Am I doing what the Bible asks: glorifying God in my body?[7]

My daily exercise regimen needs to be clearly defined. The Bible says our bodies are temples, and if we don't treat them with reverence we are failing in our worship of God.[8] Life is the first gift from God. Our bodies are life. If we don't maintain that gift, we're showing how little we appreciate what God has given us—and that's the same as showing God how little we appreciate Him.

If you give someone a gift, and they break it, or toss it aside and ignore it, it tells you they don't really care about you. Mistreating this precious gift God has given us sends the same message—to someone who's always listening.

If, on the other hand, you give someone a gift, and they say thank you every time they talk to you, and they treat it with care, and they show other

---

7   1 Corinthians 6:20.
8   1 Corinthians 3:16–17.

people how happy they are with what you gave them, then that lets you know how they feel about you, too. And it makes you want to give them more gifts.

God wants us to be happy. He wants us to enjoy the gifts He's given us. Show Him that you do.

Chapter 42

GOD'S PURPOSE EQUATION

To me, math is the pure truth. Math is the language of God. Period. It's truth. Two plus two will always equal four. Calculus is God's wonderful language.

So let's speak in God's language. Let's create a mathematical statement: P = A + S + W + C + R + KDNA.

In this equation, in this statement, P is purpose. P is what I mean to do, what I am meant to do. It is the mission, the commitment, the pledge, and the promise. What God intended me to do.

As you can see in the mathematical equation, P is the answer. It's not part of the formula for arriving at the answer. It *is* the answer. The formula tells us how to get the answer. The formula tells us how to determine what our purpose is. But the equation answers another question, a larger question, that people all over the world ask in a million different ways. The equation answers the question, What is the meaning of life?

Like the answer to a lot of the really tough questions in life, the answer is simple, but complex. It's like Einstein's Theory of Relativity. $E=MC^2$ is simple, but it describes one of the most complicated, complex, and powerful concepts in the universe.

So does this equation. God's Purpose Equation answers the question, Why am I here?

Every single one of us has a different set of traits and capacities, skills and flaws that add up to give each and every one of us a unique purpose.

When you know your true purpose, when you know your prophetic purpose, your Kingdom purpose, God's purpose for you, then you'll know the meaning of life.

The answer is different for everybody. It's like Einstein's theory that way, too. The amounts and types of things on one side of the equal sign determine the values on the other side of the equation. In the Theory of Relativity, the M, the mass—what kind and how much—determines the amount of E, or energy, you get.

In the Purpose Equation, the amounts and kinds of things you add together—that special blend of qualities and quantities you bring into the mix—determine your purpose. Every single one of us has a different set of traits and capacities, skills and flaws, that add up to give each and every one of us a unique purpose.

So what's the whole equation?

P equals purpose. A, in this mathematical statement, equals my abilities. S is my strengths. W is my weaknesses—because you must add, not subtract, your weaknesses to the equation. C is my character. R is my relationships, and KDNA is my Kingdom DNA.

So, $P = A + S + W + C + R + KDNA$.

Purpose equals my abilities, plus my strengths, plus my weaknesses, plus my character, plus my relationships, plus my Kingdom DNA.

When I put them all together, I'll be able to solve the equation and define my purpose.

Do you know your abilities? They're the obvious and the not-so-obvious talents and skills, tendencies and capacities that each of us has in varying amounts. It's not just, "I'm good at math." Or, "I know how to sew." It's also, "I can give words of encouragement," and "I make people laugh."

Can you leap tall buildings? Or build them? Supermen and architects are equally important in God's kingdom. So are people who care enough to tend to the sick, and to teach. There is room and a need for people of all different abilities in God's kingdom here on Earth. He wants cooks and CEOs, poets and presidents, surgeons and songwriters. There is no such thing as a menial job in God's kingdom.

And don't confuse the job you have with your abilities. How many actors work as waiters? How many engineers pay their way through college working in construction? Even the lucky ones who do exactly what they trained for and love have other interests and talents.

> *There is no such thing as a menial job in God's kingdom.*

Whether you're a brain surgeon with incredible dexterity and an astounding talent for saving lives or a foreman in a factory with a talent for increasing the efficiency of the production line and getting people to work together, your job is not the only thing you can do.

When a rocket scientist goes home at night, he probably doesn't build another rocket. No matter how much he loves his job. He might play saxophone with a jazz band, or coach Little League baseball.

Your job shows only one aspect of your abilities. Do you have hobbies or other skills? Can you make a cake from scratch? A dress? Do you paint? Make furniture? Play chess? Did you set up your home computer network?

Can you play piano? Write a résumé? Speak another language? Or, can you *learn* to? Not everyone can. So, if you do, that's one of your abilities. You don't have to be a professional translator to count it as one of the things you're capable of.

You have the abilities that contribute to *your* purpose, and the abilities you have will help determine what that purpose is.

Our abilities may include some of our strengths, the S in the formula. But our strengths go beyond them. They include our physical, emotional, and psychological strengths, our ability to endure, to guide, to be compassionate and steadfast. Can you throw a ball farther or run faster than your teammates? Can you be counted on to be honest and loyal? Are you trustworthy? Dedicated? Determined?

What about your spiritual strength? How strong is your faith? How strong is your worship? How strong is God in you? If we are going to ask God to be strong for us, we ought to be willing to do the same for Him. How strongly you stand with God, and for God, plays a crucial part in determining your purpose.

So do your flaws. That's why your weaknesses are counted in the equation. But they're not necessarily negatives. We all have them. We all have things we *can't* do, or things we can't do very well. They may even show up in some of our abilities. Even a great cook may not be able to keep a soufflé from falling. The world's greatest pitchers can rarely hit.

That's okay. It takes all kinds to make up the team. Nobody asks the punter on a football team to play linebacker. And, if you're aware of your weaknesses, you can work on them. The equation isn't static. It's not, "This is it. This is me. This is all I'll ever have to work with."

The equation is dynamic. The components grow and change as we grow and change. We develop our abilities, build on our strengths, and—sometimes, unfortunately, sadly, but it's true—become weaker in some aspect of our life. We may not dedicate the time to our families that they deserve. We may not try as hard on the job because we're upset about something our supervisor said or did. We may not walk as closely with God as we can, and should.

That weakens our ability to achieve our purpose. And, if you want exceedingly, abundantly, above all, you should be willing to give your all. You should try to eliminate, or at least reduce, your weaknesses. Weaken your weaknesses every day.

You can weaken your weaknesses, and you can build your character. A lot of people think character, the next part of the equation, is set. Character, they say, is how we are. They're right, and wrong. It is how we are, but it can be changed.

Character is more than our personality. It's *how* we behave, but it's also *why* we act the way we do. It's our intentions, not just our actions. To help an old lady across the street only because she needs it and you can is noble; to do it so others will notice and say how nice you are is boastful and egotistical.

But you can learn to shed your pride. You can be a better person. You can teach yourself to treat others better. You can learn to control your anger, to stop criticizing others, to offer encouragement instead of disparagement.

You can improve your good qualities, too. You can be even kinder. Even more patient. Even more helpful.

Weaken your weaknesses, and build your character. Every day.

As you do, every day, your purpose will become clearer and more powerful.

But, as you already know, you can't do it alone. Relationships, the R in the equation, are crucial. You must build your Life Surrounded, make sure all the spots are filled. You must work every day to strengthen your primary relationship, your relationship with God. And you must love, honor, and cherish your family.

Our relationships, as we discussed earlier, are vital in helping us succeed in life, fulfilling our purpose, and discovering God's rewards. Our relationships help or hinder us along the Path of Miracles.

The last part of the formula is KDNA, our Kingdom DNA—that God-given Spiritual DNA deposited within each and every one of us. We all have it, the instant we come into the world. But it's not a constant. It doesn't remain the same. It's up to each of us to activate our Spiritual DNA, those God genes, and add their power to our purpose.

We're all born with the faith gene and the worship gene and the mercy gene. But we can live counter to our DNA. We can defy the call to worship, or let our faith flag. Do that, and you diminish the power of your purpose. Do it enough, and you may never discover your true purpose.

Activate your Spiritual DNA, activate the faith of God within you by following the Kingdom Principles, and you unlock the power of KDNA and add it to the Purpose Equation.

Add all the elements together, and you discover your special purpose in life. No two will be the same. The answer is different for everyone. And our purpose will help determine our journey, and what we discover along the way.

> *Our purpose determines our path and our prism.*

That's why Mary Magdalene saw one thing and Peter and John saw something different in the empty tomb. Mary Magdalene saw the mercy seat and Peter and John saw folded linen because Mary Magdalene's purpose was different from Peter and John's.

They arrived in the same place, but they arrived with different strengths, different weaknesses, different characters, different personal narratives, battles and journeys, and different abilities. Even though they arrived at the same place, because of their differences, and because of their different purposes, they discovered different things.

That speaks to the reality that the journey, how we get there, and what we carry within us is as important as the goal, as the destination.

Scholars throughout time have said similar things. The path is as important as the destination. And what we learn as we travel that road shapes how we see and what we see when we reach that destination.

People can join us in our journey, and they can step into the same circumstance, the same situation, and they will still see something totally different.

Our purpose determines our path and our prism.

Chapter 43

PATHETIC PERCEPTION AND PROPHETIC REALITY

There is a fine line between the pathetic and the prophetic. Anything that is 99 percent true is still a lie. A deception. A fallacy. Something false. That's why there's a fine line between the prophetic and the pathetic.

If we truly want prophetic reality, we need to commit ourselves to living in 100 percent unadulterated, uncensored, unbridled truth. That means telling the truth, of course, but I go beyond that. I'm talking about *living* in truth.

Every single day, we have choices to make. Between the pathetic and the prophetic. Between the truth and the 99 percent true, which is basically a lie. Between mediocrity and excellence. Between our past and our future.

God gave man two great gifts: a way out and a way in. That's free will and salvation. Free will and grace. He gave us the ability to pick our own path, and the opportunity to find His.

Every day we find ourselves surrounded by both the pathetic and the prophetic, the curse and the blessing, the mistake and the miracle, the problem and the promise. Every single day, we get to choose between the two.

> *God gave man two great gifts: a way out and a way in.*

Pathetic perception is lying to myself. It is not acknowledging truth to myself. And lying to myself speaks to the mentality where I think I can do it all myself; where I think I can do all things without God and without others.

That's pathetic. It's lying to myself: that I can live exceedingly, abundantly, above all and achieve the dream, without God and without others.

Without running partners, and without God. Without my Kingdom DNA. Without activation. Without emptying toward nothing. Lying to myself.

But what if I commit myself to living in full truth? Where I utter the words—these scary, terrifying words: I need you. I'm incomplete without you.

Pathetic perception speaks to satisfaction. It says, "I'm satisfied." This is good enough. And we basically give up.

Pathetic perception speaks to surrendering. And we emotionally and spiritually justify our surrendering, our failure, and our lack of completion— our spiritual procrastination. We justify it with phrases like, "I did my best. I gave it my all."

Yes, but did you give it *His* all? Did you give it *His* best? Did you give it the best of those who love you, and whom God has placed in your life in order to take you the extra mile? *His* best.

Prophetic reality is righteousness, peace, and joy. It is, biblically, thy kingdom come, thy will be done.[1] Because if you live in truth, then His kingdom will come, and His will is being done. If you turn away from the pathetic perception, and you live in the prophetic reality, then you can see His kingdom of righteousness, peace, and joy, and His will be done.

What did Mary Magdalene see? Did she see her Lord and Savior abandon her? Did Mary see that the only person who had ever validated her and continuously maintained her was gone? Is this what she found: The abandonment of her security blanket, a first firewall, the liquidation of her source of income and of her self-acknowledgment, her identity clarification?

Not at all. That would have been a pathetic perception.

She walked in the tomb and, in that emptiness, she saw two angels. She saw the mercy seat. Her prophetic reality was greater than her pathetic perception.

> *If you live in truth, then His kingdom will come, and*
> *His will is being done.*

---

1   Matthew 6:9–11, King James Version.

What are the lenses we are going to put on, every single day? How are we going to view ourselves? How are we going to view our relationships? Our family? Our community? Those who surround us? How are we going to view the people and the circumstances and the opportunities that come our way? How are we going to view God?

The lenses we choose can be pathetic, or prophetic.

How many times have you heard someone say, "There was a missed opportunity"? How many times have you heard about a Hollywood starlet who read over a script and turned it down, and that script was given to someone else and that person won the Academy Award? How many times have you heard that story?

Why didn't they see it?

What happened to that Nike stock when it was introduced? And what's with that name? That old Greek name? You're kidding me—for a pair of sneakers?

But look at what it has become. Why didn't we see it?

This whole idea of a virtual community, of the Internet and cloud computing and social networking—why didn't we see it coming?

Because we had the wrong lenses on.

But there were those who did see it. There were those who could see the opportunity before them. They could see what could be.

The world is full of prophetic people who have lenses to see things that others do not. And those prophetic ones enable us to see beyond the here and now. The ability to see what others do not see, that's the difference between mastery and proficiency. Between success and survival.

And I argue that every single person who follows the Kingdom Principles will have the ability to put on their prophetic lenses. They will see opportunities where others see obstacles. They will see the miracles where others see mistakes. They will see promotion where others see problems. They will see the Path of Miracles.

That's the gift of the prophetic and not pathetic.

Chapter 44

EDITING LIFE

We have the power, when the Kingdom Principles are activated, to edit our life.

Does that mean that we get to literally remove the areas in our life that we don't want to confront or that we don't want to remember? No. They're part of it. We can edit the errors, but not necessarily the experience.

Let me explain.

God doesn't only say, "I'm going to make your future better." That's the archaic way of thinking. That's pre–empty tomb thinking. God says He's going to make our future better, brighter, and fuller. But that's not all. He also says, "And, by the way, I want to go back into your past and make sure that even the things you weren't right at and the things you failed at and your moments of pain and hurt and angst and trepidation—I'm going to show you how you benefited from each and every one of them."

That's the awesomeness of God. Not only does He give us a brilliant and dazzling future, a future that's abundantly, exceedingly, above all we ever had or expected, but He also gives us the ability, through the activation of these principles, to go back and find a better past in the past that we had.

He lets us go back and edit our life.

Editing Life means to go back to those moments that we do not want to go back to and reexamine, reevaluate, and review them—not just review in the sense of remembering, but actually *re-view* them; see them all over again, but from the whole new perspective of a life filled with the faith of God.

Editing Life is going back and going over those difficult times in your past and asking yourself, "Can I find any good in this?"

Because you can. Embedded in every single circumstance and challenge in our life, there is a piece of God. In each and every circumstance we go through, regardless of how horrific and terrible and painful it may be, He is there. God is present even in the midst of our most difficult and horrific circumstances and moments, our trials and tribulations. He is forever present.

> *God gives us the ability to find a better past in the past that we had.*

And when you realize and recognize that, when you put that in your hard drive and let it work its way through your memory, it's like an antivirus: it cleans out the bugs and lets your internal software work the way it was supposed to.

What good can you find? In the abuse? In the loss? In the car accident or the disease that took away that loved one?

We cannot always understand God's grand plan. We cannot always see why something happens or—as arrogant as it may sound when we're talking about the Almighty—agree with His methods. But, there is good even in the worst of events.

I already told you the story of the father who lost his teenage daughter to a drunk driver, about how he began a program and travels from high school to high school dramatically pointing out the terrible consequences of drinking and driving. I told you how that program, born of that horrible loss, is saving the lives of so many others.

Here's another story, of a man who lost his twenty-year-old son in an ambush in Iraq, and turned his pain into the power to save others.

Army Pvt. First Class John Hart's death devastated his father. The former College Republicans chapter president teamed with liberal Sen. Edward Kennedy to complain to Congress that U.S. soldiers fighting the war were being sent into battle without body armor.

Then he went further. He formed a company to build comparatively low-cost robotic vehicles capable of disabling roadside bombs before they kill more soldiers.

Can you tell me that there was no good in those tragic losses? I don't think so.

Editing Life provokes us to go back and, before we save the final version of that experience in our memory banks, edit it to make sure we are able to extrapolate the piece of God from every single sentence, every single paragraph.

Otherwise, we go forward with faulty programming. Our software trips over the same bugs. We get caught in constantly repeating loops that don't allow us to complete our mission in life. The bugs keep us trapped in one spot, or give us wrong answers so we end up veering off our correct path.

We have a tendency to write certain scripts in our lives based upon our experience, and we fall into certain roles. And we keep repeating those and getting nowhere until we learn to go back and edit the script so we can rewrite our future.

When we Edit Life, we're not really changing the past, we're reexamining it so that we can write our future.

Think about that man you know with the alcohol problem, or the woman in the bad relationship. What roles are they playing? What script do they have to rewrite so they can break the cycle?

As long as you repeat the roles of the past, you end up repeating the past. The actors on the stage may change, but the end will be the same. Until you go back and edit your life, you'll end up with the same result.

> *Your past empowers your present and propels your future.*

Editing Life also means looking at our present and removing the passive voice.

The passive voice is when you speak from the past rather than from your future and from your destiny. Speaking from the past is unacceptable in God's software. His software will recognize the fact that you are speaking from the past when you should be speaking from your destiny, from your empty tomb/upper room perspective, from your purpose, and from exceedingly, abundantly, above all.

Let's visit every chapter in our life. Let's go back to every paragraph to make sure there's continuity, transitional phrases. Let's not presumptuously jump the gun and leave this half-empty project, this half-empty vision, this half-empty dream on that page of our life and jump to the next one.

Our objective in editing our life narrative is removing the passive voice. Which means every single circumstance speaks to the future rather than to the hurt of the past. So that even when I speak about that divorce, I will write about what that divorce taught me. I will think and speak of it in terms of, "I learned the following from that experience. . . ."

What did that divorce give me? It gave me inner strength. It exposed the reality that I can do things for myself, that I can succeed when I thought I would fail, that I can find the courage and faith to step into the unknown. It gave me the ability to look beyond complete, total codependency and enabled me to pursue dreams that I had, that I had stored away or kept hidden, that I had never pursued because I had sacrificed myself exclusively on an altar of a marriage that had no reciprocity at all, whatsoever.

Revisiting your experiences and viewing them through that prism—the perspective of "What did they give me? What did I gain?"—permits you to find the power that they gave you to make your *now* active.

Viewed from that perspective, your past empowers your present and propels your future. It allows you to make your present active, not passive. Things won't happen *to* you, you make them happen. You don't wait for things to come your way, you run toward them. You no longer drift through life, you know where you are going and you know how to get there.

So, look at every single experience. Revisit every chapter. Remove the passive voice. Get rid of the fragments. Eliminate the incomplete sentences. Create fluidity. Insert transitional phrases. But make sure that every single one of them identifies the nugget and the principal and the God piece, the God factor, in each and every single experience.

Let's create a viable outline that makes sense: Coherent. Persuasive. Powerful. Engaging. Let's make sure we have the right descriptors. Let's make sure our narrative is rich, and that it's not dull.

Edit life. Put the final period on it—and exclamation point if necessary! Make sure you've done your due diligence successfully, and that syntactically and semantically there's fluidity and coherency and viable articulation in our personal narrative. Then make sure that you save your narrative and it's protected in your memory. That way, you will lock in the script that empowers your present and puts you on the path to a future filled with promise and purpose.

Chapter 45

CLOSING THE CHAPTER

God will never bless the next chapter in one's life until all areas are in order in the current chapter.

That doesn't mean you can't move forward, that you can't step to the next rung on the ladder, that you can't move forward in the book of your life. You can. But you're wasting your time.

You *can* move forward in writing the next chapter, but the book will never be published until you go back and finalize the previous one. Go ahead. Jump the page. Jump the chapter. Jump three chapters. You got writer's block here, so you figure you'll just skip over it and start the next chapter. Hey, it happens. It has happened to me. Jump the page. But it won't be published. It won't be distributed. No one's going to read it. It's incomplete.

If you try to step to the next rung of the ladder without God's blessing on this one, it's not guaranteed that you will slip and fall. But it is guaranteed that you won't get to the top of the ladder.

If you try to move on to the next chapter of your life without putting everything in order in this one, your success—the exceedingly, abundantly, above all success component—will not be activated. Survival, yes. Success, no. Failure, probably. You may walk out with a manuscript, but since it won't be complete, it won't be published.

> *Forgiveness is the period at the end of the sentence, and*
> *at the end of the chapter.*

That's why we need to confront the obstacles and bring some closure to those chapters before we move on.

Now, I want to make it clear that by *confrontation* I don't mean you go back to that husband who beat the living daylights out of you, or that person who dealt drugs, or that father who abandoned you, and you *physically* confront them. It doesn't mean you have to go back to them and say, "Now I'm going to bring an end to this chapter. Now I'm going to tell you how miserable you made my life. And now I forgive you, and now I release you."

I don't mean physically. I mean *spiritually*—and, through *that* means, psychologically and emotionally. You need to do this *before* the throne room in heaven, that holy place where God sits upon His throne.[1] At times, if you so desire and it is beneficial to you, you may want to have a physical closure. It is not required. What is required is for you, with God and in God, to bring these chapters to closure.

For those traumatic situations, those hurtful situations and egregious situations in life, forgiveness is the period at the end of the sentence, and at the end of the chapter.

> *Celebration and repentance go hand in hand.*

How can I be certain that God has blessed this chapter, or will bless the next chapter? How do I know that I've got this chapter wrapped up?

Ask yourself: did I acknowledge my mistakes in this chapter? Did I learn from my mistakes in this chapter? Did I celebrate my successes in this chapter? Because celebration and repentance go hand in hand.

It's not all some sort of continual, purging, sacrificial, noncelebratory sort of scrutinizing of the negatives. It's not an opaque presentation. You *should* celebrate your successes. Did you celebrate your success with others? Did you forgive? And were you forgiven? Did you give honor? Did you serve someone else's dream while building your own? Did you leave more than what you took? Can you say, "Well done"? And can God say, "Well done!"?

We know when it's right. We know. We know when it's right to move on. We know when we turn our eyes away so that we don't look at the things we left unfinished. We know when we're washing our cars that we really didn't want to get into every little corner in there and get it to shine and get all the

---

1 Revelation 4:1–11.

dust out and all the dirt. We know and we hope that someone else doesn't see that blemish. But if we try to go past that and we've been untrue to ourselves and we have been untrue to God, sooner or later we have to come back and make sure that it's really clean.

But I must do it in partnership. Because I'll be absolutely honest with you, no matter how hard I try to detail my car, I *always* fall short. I never pick up everything in every nook and cranny. There are things that are left between the seats and in certain spots, and there are things, to be frank, that I just don't *want* to pick up. There are some horrible things that have been left behind for so long that I just don't want to pick them up. I mean, honestly, how old can that smudge spot really be? There are things in my life that I just don't want to pick up.

That's where that strategic partnership with God first kicks in. He is the master detailer. He will take care.

But here's what it requires: it requires me to point to it. To say, "By the way, can you come here? You see that spot? I don't want to pick that up. It's too traumatic. It's too painful. It's hard to see it, to tell the truth. It's underneath the seat, on the right-hand side. It's there. Can you take care of that for me?"

And He will. He's the master at doing that very thing.

Chapter 46

ORDER PRECEDES PROMOTION

The truth is, we find out later in life that the journey *was* the destination.

So even when we arrive at the same point, because of our different journeys, we find different things. You can't see what I see.

It's like you really can't have what I have, even if I wanted to give it to you. You would have to go through what I went through, embody what I embody, suffer what I have suffered. We each have to identify our different roads and journeys, identify the individuals and the relationships that make up our running partners in life and put everything in order, in order to see exceedingly, abundantly, above all.

> *Conflict will always arise in our lives when something is not in perfect order.*

Order is so important. I really can't emphasize it enough! In everything from subatomic particles and microscopic entities to the greatest of stars, planets, and the vastness of God's wonderful universe, there is order. There is order in the process. There is order in the programs. There is order in the systems. There is order in the institutions. There is order of unity. There is always *order*.

It needs to be the same in our lives.

What do I mean? What is the set of metrics for checking whether my life is in order?

First, am I doing everything with integrity? That's number one. And you and I both know what integrity means: In my work and my finances and my family, is there anything I'm hiding from them? Is there anything that I am not being totally honest about? Am I lying? Is there any sort of deception or lie?

Second, am I giving more than I receive? Even at work. Whatever it may be, am I giving more than I receive?

Third, am I preparing the way for someone to be more successful than me in the future? Am I guaranteeing someone else's success? Beyond me? Beyond now?

Fourth, am I being a good steward of my environment? I don't mean just my corporate environment—I mean my earthly environment, my spiritual environment, my emotional environment. Am I creating or facilitating an atmosphere that's positive, that's productive, that edifies, enriches, and empowers?

And fifth, am I honoring God? My family? Myself?

> *There are consequences to disorder.*

That's what we mean by order—dealing with the details.

If we don't, the consequences will impact every aspect of our lives. Conflict will always arise in our lives when something is not in perfect order. Perfect, though, doesn't mean without *any* flaw; it means perfect alignment— a vertical and horizontal alignment. God will take care of ironing out the wrinkles and removing the stains.

So, even when you have someone like Donald Trump, someone who has incredible business acumen and success, in his relationships, with respect to marriages and family, you can still find that there isn't perfect order. You can still have conflict.

Is it a coincidence that Donald went through his bankruptcy, his economic disarray, right about the time that his family and his marriage were not in order?

No. These things are all related.

The notion that my spiritual life can be in disarray, yet my finances, my relationships, my marriage, my work, my career will be in perfect order— it's not going to happen. There are consequences to disorder. Disorder, in fact, is a type of sin arising from Adam and Eve's expulsion from the Garden of Eden.

The opposite of order would be chaos, anarchy. And when we have spiritual chaos, relational chaos, it will transfer to the other parts of our life. We will see the places where we have order affected. And if we don't tend to the area where the trouble started, everything in our life can disintegrate into chaos. Into anarchy. Into disarray.

It's Organizational Management and Behavior 101. It's not obsessive-compulsive order. But it is order.

Let's take care of this area. Let's take care of this other area. When you don't, when you jump from one area to the next, when you jump from one relationship to the next, then to the next, then you just end up with a history of unfulfilled relationships, of broken dreams, of unfulfilled promises. You have a history of violations and misdemeanors.

We need to learn to place things in order.

It begins with the spirit world first. Let's not pretend. It's spirit first. It's Kingdom first. Earth second. Not the other way around.

You have to place yourself in line spiritually first. You have to align yourself in the place where whatever area you can't place in order, God does. It's not entirely up to you. You don't have to put *everything* in your life in order, all by yourself, to achieve the next level of attainment. But you must be strategically located in a place of order. He'll take care of the rest.

> *God will take care of ironing out the wrinkles and removing the stains.*

We already saw that one of the things we have to empty ourselves of is our raging auto-dependency, our out-of-control self-dependency. We can't do it all ourselves.

We have to work with God to put order in our lives. It's not all me on my own, and it's definitely not just leaving it all up to God. I do, with God. I do have to do things with integrity, give more than I receive, honor God and my family. I do have to deal with the details. But wherever the details arise where I do not have the wherewithal, the courage, the time, the discipline, or the commitment to put in order for myself, that's when the God gene kicks in. When I have anxiousness or I have trepidation, God will step in.

But I must authorize God. This does challenge general theological beliefs—it's even sacrilegious to a degree to some—but we must authorize

God. Here's the biblical and the spiritual and the cosmic reality of this. It speaks to the notion of free will. It speaks to the idea, as many Greek philosophers throughout history have depicted, that God knows our destiny but He allows us to choose our path.

It is God touching our touchscreen. It is God, putting His signature on the card. It is God's signature process and we say, Yes, we authorize.

If we permit God to help us, if we authorize God to step in in the areas and the relationships where we are experiencing difficulty dealing with the details, then we place things in order.

To be honest with you, many individuals never live exceedingly, abundantly, above all, because they are still living in deception in some areas of their lives. They're 99 percent there—but there's an area there that is literally out of order: it's not working. So they never find that they are already running in the Path of Miracles.

Why? Because order precedes promotion.

Mary Magdalene, Peter, and John were promoted as a result of their experiences on the third day, of discovering the empty tomb and meeting Jesus, and then the subsequent encounters with Christ throughout the forty days that he roamed Jerusalem and other parts of Israel after his resurrection. They were promoted to the position of founding pillars of the Church of Jesus Christ. They went from being followers to being leaders—of a worldwide religion.

They literally entered into the major, major leagues. They were privates and they became generals. Because they came, they saw, they experienced, and they put things in order.

Once you have your life in order, once you have order in that specific chapter, once you are able to see the mercy seat, once you are able to see that perfect order, then you, too, can proceed to transformation.

PRINCIPLE SIX

THERE IS TRANSFORMATION, FOLLOWED BY RECOGNITION

Chapter 47

CHANGE YOURSELF;
CHANGE YOUR LIFE

Grace always runs toward mercy. Love always runs toward peace. Faith always runs toward hope. To run away from problems is one thing, but to run toward promises is another. To pray for God to change our circumstances is one thing, but to ask God to change us so we can prevail is another.

That's a Kingdom notion: Don't ask that the world be changed for you; you have to be the one to change it.

This archaic idea that the things around me have to be changed for me— it doesn't work that way. *We* need to change. We are the ones who need to change in order to deal with our current circumstances, our current reality. Transformation of the outside will only occur when there's transformation of the inside. Internal transformation precedes an external transformation. Personal transformation precedes corporate transformation.

> *Don't ask that the world be changed for you; you have to be the one to change it.*

Recently, among the issues we've dealt with at some of the think tank meetings that I attend, we've discussed the challenge of global warming. My position has been: We're never going to be able to succeed in addressing the issue of global warming, we're never going to succeed in addressing the issue of climate change in our atmosphere, so long as our personal atmosphere is polluted. We've got to clear up our personal atmosphere, I've got to clean up my personal atmosphere, if we want to clear up the atmosphere around us.

Of course I'm speaking metaphorically, but the reality remains. What am I polluting the air with? Am I polluting it with negative ideas? Am I polluting it with condescending terms? Am I polluting it with hatred and envy and jealousy and criticism? What am I polluting my environment with?

Whenever I am able to address my personal atmosphere and bring clarity to it, and address this ozone layer and gas and the ultraviolet rays that are impacting me because I have damaged the protective ingredients of the atmosphere, then I can deal corporately and communally with what is happening in my physical world. But we must deal with our spiritual reality before we deal with the physical reality.

We are spiritual beings first. What we see in the physical world is a reflection of what's occurring in our spiritual world. If we are going to transform our physical world, we must first make sure that our spiritual world has been transformed. If we want to see heaven on Earth, to see His kingdom come, His will be done,[1] then we have to transform ourselves and follow His Kingdom Principles.

> *What we see in the physical world is a reflection of what's occurring in our spiritual world.*

When we want to change our lives, we must first change ourselves.

Rather than ask God to give me a better job, I'd ask God to help me be a better person, a better worker. To assist me in becoming better. Instead of asking God to do everything for me, I'd say, "God, I'm going to depend on you. I'm going to meet you halfway. But I'm willing to do my part."

Remember, Mary Magdalene did not stay home. She didn't sit waiting for God to bring her the answer. She ran. And Christ came from the dead and visited Mary Magdalene at that moment.

Mary Magdalene met him halfway.

We have this inclination in our lives, we have this propensity, we have this affinity for thinking it has to come top-down. It doesn't. Never throughout this relationship between heaven and Earth has there ever been an understanding that God would do it all and mankind would just sit back and reap the blessings.

---

1   Matthew 6:10.

Some of us are showered with blessings, and we don't appreciate them. Instead of applying Kingdom Principles in our lives, we take those gifts for granted. My friend Everardo Zavala knows what happens then.

Everardo grew up in a family of four, and while education was stressed at home, he never really tried to get into a university. But a high school counselor unilaterally filled out the college application for him and, later, one of his professors encouraged him to go to law school.

Did he recognize his blessings? Did he give thanks? No. Not even when he passed the California bar on his first sitting.

He landed a well-paying job right away, and promptly set about squandering his money and his life as fast as he could, with trips to Mexico and Las Vegas, on women and booze.

But through it all, he felt empty. He had money, a job, and his guilty pleasures, but not happiness.

Then one day, he lost it all on a business venture, and was nearly killed when his car slammed into a center divider. As he was recovering, the woman who raised him, his grandmother, died.

Luckily, he saw his circumstances for what they were: a wake-up call. He realized that he had tried doing everything on his own, and for himself. Now, he says, "My sole focus is on serving and helping others' dreams and visions come to pass, and thereby disrupt society's image of money-hungry attorneys—sharks with briefcases, to be exact."

And now, he's finding himself on the Path of Miracles. Opportunities are opening up. He's winning generous settlements for his clients without even having to go to trial.

"God has connected me with powerful men and women of God who care more about me as a man of God than they do of the attorney," he says. "Through the nurturing of these relationships, doors have swung wide open in the national political arena, as well as in the entertainment industry. My clients range from Grammy Award winners to film industry moguls. God has also granted me favor in the educational arena by extending me a professorship position in the nation's leading Christian law school."

We have to meet God halfway. It is our responsibility, and we need to take responsibility. If we get to that point of convergence, to the nexus, then He will meet us at that point.

It was Mary Magdalene standing up, rising up in the midst of darkness with perfume and fragrance and scents, and running to that tomb that brought her to discover the miracle of the resurrection. If she had not assumed responsibility, it would not have happened.

We need to do the same. We need to stand up. We are the ones who are responsible.

So don't say, "Lord, please change the things around me." We need to say, "Change *me* so I can change those things." The true power of change is within us. We are the power of change.

You know, we make these audacious prayers: "God, change the circumstances." Well, forgive me for being presumptuous and attempting to speak for Him, but let me give you in twenty-first-century vernacular what I think the Lord would say, based upon His Scripture. He would say:

"I've already equipped you to change the things around you. I've given you the DNA. I've given you the ingredients.[2] I've given you the wherewithal and the fortitude and the acumen to change the things around you.[3]

"You're asking me to do something that I've already equipped you to do. And I'm not going to do the work for you. I will be your cheerleader. And I'll be here just in case you fall. And if you fall I will pick you up.[4] But I'm not going to change the things around you for you. You change them. I made you so you can change them.[5] I made you for the rough place. I made you for the darkest hour. I equipped you to be right there in the middle of it, to be the crevice in the middle of the rock. I made you to be that dynamite to blow through things in the most difficult moments. I made you that way. Do it."[6]

So every time we call out to God and say, "Please change things for me," I believe that it is an insult to God. It's a lack of acknowledgment of His work in our lives.

Yes, we want a bigger house. Yes, we want to be more financially secure. Yes, we want a better job. But you can't have a better house and a better car and a better job until there is a better *you!*

> *The true power of change is within us. We are the power of change.*

---

2   Luke 17:21.
3   Job 22:28; Matthew 17:20.
4   Hebrews 13:5; Genesis 28:15; Genesis 21:22.
5   Ecclesiastes 9:10; Matthew 9:29.
6   Ephesians 6:14–17.

You can't have those things until you yourself have reached that point where you've learned to run while it's dark, where you acknowledge there is an empty tomb before a filled upper room, where you learn to run in concert with someone else, where you put your life in order.

Once you do those things, then you can have the bigger house and the better car and job. But I would argue this: After you have done those things you won't say, "Give me a better house." Because then you'll understand that better houses and better cars are residual by-products of the natural picture.

The natural picture is: I found my upper room. My DNA just kicked in by doing justice and making sure that the generation that follows me is greater than myself. I'm helping others in their darkest hour. I'm running with someone else. Once those things come in, you won't have to ask for the bigger house and better car and job.

The Bible says, "Seek ye first the kingdom of God and His righteousness and all these things shall be added unto you."[7]

This is the add-on. The better house, the nicer car, the job—these are all add-ons. These are the extras. The problem is that many of us see them as the principal goal. We look at the residual by-products as the primary objective, when they're actually residual by-products.

Seek first His kingdom. Then you won't have to ask for those things. You'll have them.

Instead of asking for those things, I should be asking myself: Am I changing the world? Am I leaving an imprint? Am I doing good? Am I doing justice? Am I helping others?

What's my legacy? That I had a better job? That I had a better car? That I had a bigger house? I sure hope not! I want my legacy to be that I made my world a better place. That others are doing better and will continue to do even better. That the ones who follow me will be greater than me. Yes, I want to live exceedingly, abundantly, above all. But even more than that, I want everyone else to live exceedingly, abundantly, above all, too.

---

7   Matthew 6:33, King James Version.

Chapter 48

GOD CHANGE

Y̶ou will reign over the very thing that held you back. The Bible says so.[1] The narrative of the empty tomb tells us so.

In the Bible, Matthew describes how Mary Magdalene found the tomb open. The rock that had been set in place to seal it had been rolled out of the way, and an angel was sitting on it.

Think about it: The stone is removed and now an angel is sitting on the stone that held the master back. The stone that held life back, that stone, there was an angel sitting on it. He sat upon the thing that held life back. In the same way, you will sit upon the things that held your life back.

By the way, in Kingdom terms, when you sit upon a stone, it means you reign over it. You have authority and dominion over it. It can no longer hold you back. It can no longer speak into you. It can no longer captivate you. It can no longer obstruct you. It is conquered. It is under your complete and utter control.

> *You will reign over the very thing that held you back.*

After they buried Jesus, they placed a stone in front of the tomb to safeguard Christ's body in the sepulcher. That stone was carved from a mountain. The fact that the stone was part of a mountain means that the stone was part of God.

I'll explain:

Let's go back to Genesis. If you adhere to the creation story, or at least if

---

1   John 20.

you have some affinity toward it, who created the wonderful heavens and the earth? The Good Lord.

Well, if the Good Lord created the heavens and the earth that means He created that mountain the stone was carved from, which of course means He created that stone as well.

That very earth, that mountain that He created, is now the instrument holding him back. What does that symbolize for us? It shows us that, many times, the things that hold us back are of our very own creation.

In the vast majority of circumstances in our lives we are held back by the very circumstances we created. Christ was in a tomb. He was on the side of a mountain that was created by God, in a tomb that was created by God.

The vast majority of obstacles that hold us back are of our own creation. The very things that we are held back by are things that we've created throughout our journey. And because we created them, we already have the ability to remove them. We have the authority to remove them—because we know their DNA.

And once we remove them, we reign over them. We have dominion.

> *Many times, the things that hold us back are of our very own creation.*
> *And because we created them, we have the ability to remove them.*

The angel sat on the rock. Then Mary Magdalene encounters Christ outside the tomb. But she doesn't recognize him. As a matter of fact, the Bible says she thinks he's the gardener. She doesn't recognize him.[2]

That's another lesson for us now: When people no longer recognize who you are, that means you have been transformed. And when I say that they no longer recognize you, I mean that your actual physical appearance will change dramatically.

When you apply Kingdom Principles in your life and activate your Spiritual DNA, you appear at peace with yourself—because you are. Your attitude will change—you'll be happier and more confident—and the way you carry yourself will be totally different. And that will spill over into other areas of your life. You might lose a lot of weight, or start working out or running and

---

2   John 20:14.

look more fit than you did before. Or you might step up to the plate on that big project at work instead of hanging back and letting others take the lead. Or, you might do all of the above. But the change will be so profound that you will be transformed. People who know you will say, "My goodness, you've changed!" People who haven't seen you in a while will do a double take and say, "Is that really you?"

Transformation to such a degree that it becomes difficult for those who know you to recognize you is God transformation and God change.

And you know what? If it becomes difficult for those around you to recognize you, it usually becomes difficult for you to recognize yourself. That's God change.

If you think you've changed but they can recognize you right away, without any sort of trepidation or any sort of difficulty, then it's not God change. You may have changed. You may have made a very positive change. You may have made a necessary change. You may have taken a step on the way to God change. But it's not God change.

Who changes you? Is it your circumstances? Is it God? Or is it *you*? All three can change you. But who transforms you? Only one brings about the sort of transformation experienced on that third day. Only God transformation can bring about that reaction from people that makes them say, "My goodness! I can't believe it's you."

> *The Kingdom Principles change us to such a degree that*
> *we're no longer the same.*

Most people don't want to go that far. And most of the people around us don't want to see us change so much that they don't recognize us. At least, that's what they think now.

That's because most people are afraid of change. What's worse: they're afraid to admit it! The status quo is so safe. But without transformation, without change, we're in the tomb. We're in the tomb of stagnation. We're in the tomb of mediocrity. We're in the melancholy tomb. We're in a tomb of rituals, habits, and traditions that lead us nowhere.

So even if we think the people around us don't want us to change, when they see that the change is for the good, they'll be happy. I would speculate that those around us would embrace a radical transformation, as long as it's for good. As long as it comes with honor, with greater love, with joy, with greater authenticity.

The same was true of Mary Magdalene, Peter, and John. None of the disciples wanted to see Jesus change at first. None of them wanted him to die. But he knew he had to undergo that radical transformation, from earthly flesh to heavenly spirit, to ascend to sit with his Father—The Father, OUR Father. So he went to the cross.

And even after he had died, the disciples weren't ready for him to change. Mary Magdalene went to the tomb to put fragrances and perfumes on Christ's body. And when she didn't find him there, in the tomb where he had been laid, she cried. And the angels she saw on the mercy seat asked her why—after all, why should she be crying? The greatest miracle of all had just happened, and she's unhappy!

We can probably understand why she's crying at that moment. She didn't know what had happened. She didn't understand. All she knew was that Christ's body was missing.

But a few moments later, she meets Jesus outside the tomb, and even after he clears up her confusion and she realizes who he is, she *still* doesn't want him to change. She tries to hold him back, to keep him there with her, the way he was, in his fleshly form. Jesus has to tell her, "Stop clinging to me, for I have not yet ascended to my Father."[3]

He was telling her that, changed as he was, he wasn't finished, so she shouldn't try to stop him. Instead, she should be happy for him, and go tell all the other disciples the great news: He was back and he was better than ever.

After your transformation, so are you. Better than ever. You're a new and improved you. It is Life 2.0. Oh, yes, 1.0 was good. But 2.0 is better. It's faster. It's more productive. It's richer. It's cleaner. It's purer. And it's easier, by the way. It's not as complicated as it used to be.

The Kingdom Principles change us to such a degree that we're no longer the same. We're better. Life is easier. Things are greater, more abundant. Not *enough*. Not *sufficient*. Exceedingly, abundantly, above all. Jesus said, "I came that they may have life, and have it abundantly."[4]

---

3 John 20:17.
4 John 10:10.

As I mentioned at the beginning of this book, he didn't say anything about us having to wait for it. He said "life abundant." That abundance, the treasures and rewards God has for us, exists right here. It's not only in the afterlife. No. No. No. No and no. Did I emphasize *no*?

The fact of the matter is that the Bible says, "Thy kingdom come, thy will be done *on Earth* as it is in heaven."[5]

Why do we have to wait to die to live abundantly? Why do we have to wait to die to see God? Why do we have to wait to die to experience full joy? Why do we have to wait to die to live exceedingly, abundantly, above all?

All of these things are for here. Right here. Right now.

> *After your transformation, life is better than ever. It's richer, easier, purer, and more abundant.*

Jesus said if I follow him I am guaranteed eternal life. I am guaranteed that life will go on. That after death, there is life. That my soul will not die. My spirit will continue. That my consciousness and my senses will live forevermore through Christ, and in Christ.

I can see God's kingdom here on Earth. I can experience God's love, and His riches. The Kingdom Principles activate heaven so that we can *live* heaven right here. We can experience what we perceive to be a heaven here on Earth.

Thy kingdom come. Thy will be done. On Earth. That's what the Bible says.

---

5   Matthew 6:10, King James Version.

Chapter 49

YOUR LANGUAGE WILL CHANGE

The Bible describes how, after Jesus had resurrected, his disciples gathered again in the upper room where they had had the Last Supper. And, in Acts 2 it says, "they were all filled with the Holy Spirit and began to speak with other tongues."[1]

That means they spoke other languages.

Now, the Bible says there were about one hundred twenty people in the room at the time, "from every nation under heaven." They were from everywhere, and they all spoke different languages.

The Bible says they had come together there in Jerusalem because it was the Pentecost. Jews from various parts of the Middle East were gathered in that place. Not only Jews, by the way, but there were Gentiles there, too, who did not speak the Hebrew or the Aramaic tongue. Romans and Greeks were there. The Syrians were there. There were many other cultures that were gathered in that place, but the Bible says that when the one hundred twenty who were gathered in the upper room began to speak, that everyone began to hear their own language. They all understood. In fact, Acts 2:6 says, they "were bewildered because each one of them was hearing them speak in his own language."

Well, get ready. Because after we have our empty tomb experience, after we have our own upper room experience, after we recognize our purpose and undergo our transformation, our language will change, too.

When we experience our transformation, we will speak a language that everyone around us will be able to understand. We will speak a universal language.

---

1 Acts 2:4.

> *After our transformation we will speak in ways that everyone will understand, and in ways that will make them want to change, too.*

Does that mean that you will suddenly be able to speak Portuguese or Russian or Chinese? No. And I don't mean that when we speak in English, someone who only speaks Japanese will understand our words. But they *will* understand our meaning. Because I'm not speaking about earthly language, I'm talking about the language of their narratives and the language of their journey. We will speak into the lives of those around us, regardless of the language they speak.

You will have the ability and the authority and the experience and the blessing of God, where you can speak to the poor and the rich. Where you can speak to the high and the low, to the black and the white. Where you can speak the language of those who are single, or those who are married, or those who are divorced.

After we undergo our transformation, we can speak to all the different variations in God's mosaic. And we can impact every single one around us, regardless of sex or class or creed. Because we will receive this unbelievable gift of speaking to everyone without exclusion.

We will speak through our words and through our actions, through our sentiments and through our values—in ways that everyone will understand, and in ways that will make them want to change, too.

A true upper room experience will allow us to speak to our communities, to our families, to our marriages, and to lead them to the Path of Miracles as well. God gives us the language to take the persons around us, regardless of who they are and where they come from, to their upper room experience.

RECOGNIZING YOUR PURPOSE

What were you born for? What is the destiny you were meant to fulfill? What is your purpose in God's grand plan?

Mary Magdalene, Peter, and John discovered their purposes on their darkest day.

You, too, will discover your purpose when you run while it is dark, when you run even when fear is next to you. When you run toward empty. When you find the empty tomb waiting, just before your filled upper room. When you put order in your life. And when you walk out of that tomb, it will be difficult for those who know you to recognize you. That's when you discover your purpose.

You may discover you were on the path but didn't see where it really led or how you should follow it. You may see that you need to go on a different path because your purpose is revealed to you. You recognize it this way.

I'll tell you how it happened to me.

I told you already about my televangelist and Martin Luther King Jr. on the TV epiphany—about how I heard that small voice telling me that I would be used to spread the Good News.

But, hey, I was fourteen. So I ignored it. I had no inclination of being a preacher. I was a nerdy fourteen-year-old kid with one destination in mind: computer engineering—living rich, and living the American dream.

That's the path I thought I was on. But my Path of Miracles was on another route, and God insisted on making sure I knew it.

I didn't tell anybody about my TV epiphany, but right after that night, crazy things began to happen. I mean really abnormal experiences. I went to a church service and there was a person speaking into the microphone who had never been to our church before. And he stops the song in the middle of the song and he says, "There is a Samuel in here."

Now, he doesn't know me. But in my mind, this was like one of those Vegas acts—how many Samuels must there be? There's always a Samuel.

But on that day I was the only one. So everybody pointed to me.

And this person said, "Samuel, let me tell you what God told me to share with you. He said, 'Samuel, this is what I'm going to do with you. I'm going to build a platform, and I'm going to place you on that platform. It's all going to be for my glory, but I have great destiny for you. And I'm going to use you to touch so many lives. And people are going to be healed, not just of their physical ailments but of their spiritual and emotional ailments. You're going to be used to restore lives and to restore broken dreams and to inspire people. Not only that, but I'm going to make you a leader among your people.'"

So that resonated with what I had seen on TV, which nobody but me knew.

Then it happened again three months later, with someone completely different. And again.

Oh, I kept doubting what was happening. I kept trying to be that computer engineer, and God kept on trying to get me to recognize my true purpose.

And I'm going to tell you how many times it happened: forty-four times. That's why I do what I do.

I'm a Thomas who became a Peter, who became a John. That was my journey. That's how I recognized my purpose.

Mary Magdalene, Peter, and John all recognized their purposes and they were promoted from private to general. They went from being followers of Christ to being leaders of his church. From being those who listened to his words to those who spread the word.

When you recognize your purpose you, too, will be promoted.

When you fully activate your purpose then you can embrace it with passion and with promise—because you're not only activating your purpose, you're activating your passion and your promise.

Your purpose, your passion, and your promise are fully activated when you follow each of the steps of the Kingdom Principles. The answer to God's Purpose Equation becomes dazzlingly clear—brilliantly, sparklingly, luminously, radiantly clear. You *know*.

Look at what happened outside that tomb on that morning. On that third day after Christ was buried, Mary Magdalene saw him and didn't recognize him. But, after he spoke to her, she did—she recognized him, and she understood what she was supposed to do. She knew that her purpose was to inform the other disciples, and prepare them for Christ's return.

After you have your empty tomb experience, after you undergo your transformation, you, too, will recognize your purpose.

> *Your purpose, your passion, and your promise are fully activated when you follow the Kingdom Principles.*

Christ was resurrected, but so was Peter, who was dead spiritually and emotionally. Peter was dead. Not in the physical sense. But in his darkest hour, his hopes and dreams and aspirations were dead.

But by Christ coming out and Peter discovering folded linen and order—and order preceding promotion and recognition and transformation—the fact is that Peter was transformed. Peter was resurrected. And he was transformed.

He was no longer Peter the denier. The next time we see Peter, right after he comes out of the tomb and has his encounter with Christ, in the next chapter, of course, they make amends. Christ asks him, "Do you love me?" Three times. "*Aphilos, aphilos, agape.*" Do you love me? Do you love me? Do you love me? And Peter says, "Yes, I do."[1]

Okay, it's a clean slate. Thank you very much, Peter. Who's next?

Next we see Peter in the upper room and Peter stands out. This is the Peter who denied and hid in the shadows and cowered. Now he's standing out. Why is he standing out? Because he saw. He found the folded linen. Peter was resurrected.

When Christ resurrected, he was transformed. In your resurrection, in your transfiguration, your relationships, families, finances, goals, strategies, and aspirations all resurrect.

Plus, your transformation is contagious. You can't be vibrant and living, and dying to live, and alive and living in 100 percent truth, and living with

---

1   John 21:15–17.

the fullness of his resurrection, and have others around you stay the same. From businesses to entities, it all changes once you change. The transformation is complete.

It is radical transformation. And it doesn't need to be immediate. But it will provoke three things:

It will provoke the Thomases to want to touch you, to believe it's you.[2] It will provoke the Peters to step out from the boat and make it,[3] stripped from their past, and to pray for a restoration. And it will prepare you for your daybreak.

---

2   John 20:24–28.
3   Matthew 14:29–30.

Chapter 51

DAYBREAK

In the beginning of this book we talked about Mary Magdalene running just before daybreak and preparing for her own, personal daybreak. Now we're getting to the end, and to daybreak again.

After your transformation, you will discover the miracle, the treasure that God had waiting for you. That's the daybreak. Your day has come. Your day of victory, self-awareness, identity clarification, purpose clarification, healing, restoration, transfiguration, enlightenment, and renewal has come.

At your daybreak you will discover the rewards God had waiting for you, and they will enable you to live exceedingly, abundantly, above all. You will discover that God never answers our prayers. No. He doesn't. Not the way *you* want Him to.

There's nothing in Scripture that says God answers what we ask for. It says that He answers exceedingly, abundantly, above all we could ever imagine or ask for.[1] It never says that if you ask God for a hamburger, He's going to give you a hamburger.

It doesn't. It says that if you ask God for a hamburger and it's part of His will, and it's going to be beneficial for you and for His kingdom, He won't give you a hamburger—He'll give you the double burger with all your favorite fixings, the toasted buns, fries, and a thick, creamy shake. It says that no matter what you ask God for, He'll give you exceedingly, abundantly, above all you ever wanted or could have imagined.[2]

If you pray for a house, you're not going to get a house—you'll get a house with a swimming pool in the backyard. He's going to give you your house. Yeah. But He doesn't stop there. If you ask Him for a house, don't be

---

1 Ephesians 3:20.
2 Ephesians 3:20.

surprised when you see the pool and the dog and the car. Because it's *exceedingly, abundantly, above all.*

That's what happens when you activate the Kingdom Principles. If you incorporate these principles into your life, and activate them in your life, you will find your daybreak, and you will receive your rewards—exceedingly, abundantly, above all.

If you pray for your child to be saved and delivered from addiction, not only will your child be saved, but your children and your grandchildren and your grandchildren's children will also be saved.

It's activation. That's what it takes. Your treasures are already there. They exist. They literally exist in the spiritual cosmic reality. In this spiritual domain there is a God who is active, who is involved, but within the parameters of free will. And all we need to do is activate. Turn things on.

But there is no activation without revelation. First there's revelation, then there's activation, then saturation—revelation, activation, daybreak.

> *God answers exceedingly, abundantly, above all we*
> *could ever imagine or ask for.*

Prepare for your daybreak.

Let's go back to the Bible. It is, at the moment of resurrection, daybreak. We find the angels sitting on the stone at daybreak. We find Peter, later on, swimming, precisely at daybreak. At daybreak, Jesus appears.[3] Isn't it amazing? He always appears at daybreak. The Son rises, and the sun rises. That's what makes it daybreak.

Daybreak is always significant in the Bible. Jacob fought with the angel until daybreak, and he changed his name from Jacob to Israel.[4] Hence he wore a blessing scar. That blessing scar spoke volumes: not only of what he went through, but of who he fought. It was a badge of honor: I fought with God and I won.

The sun rises at every daybreak, offering a new day, and a new opportunity. Offering a clean start. It rises announcing that the nighttime is now over.

---

3   John 20:14.
4   Genesis 35:10.

Let's renew ourselves, so the iniquities of the night, the shame of the evening, are left behind. Let's celebrate the day. It brings freshness, a new beginning, and newness.

That's important. Let's not forget one thing about Christ's tomb: It was new. The Bible says it was never used before.[5] Joseph of Arimathea, who was the owner of the tomb, this rich businessman, never used it before.

Underline the word "new." That's what the Bible says, new.

When Christ went into Jerusalem in what we celebrate as the triumphant Palm Sunday entry, he rode on a colt.[6] Not on a mighty warhorse, but a colt. What kind of colt was it? It was new. Read it. It says it. It was never used before.

Well, is it a coincidence that everything that Christ enjoyed riding on, or stepping into, or being at, was new? I don't think so.

And I don't think it's a coincidence that he is resurrected, that he comes to life anew, at daybreak.

Let's give God something new every day.

The Bible says, "His mercies are new every morning."[7] Let's return the favor. Let's give God something new every day. Let's give those around us something new every day. Let's give our community, our region, and our world something new every day. A new idea. A new dream. A new hope. A new aspiration.

Whenever we introduce something new, you can almost see God smiling, and hear Him saying: "That's my boy. That's my girl."

That's the Creator in each and every one of us. He would have us do new things. It provokes God to come in—into us, and into those around us.

So let's give God something new every day. He showers us with gifts and goodness and grace, miracles and mercies and abundance, every day. We should show Him we know what to do with what He gives us. We should take those gifts out into the world and share them with others, just as Jesus shared the miracle of resurrection, of everlasting, eternal life, with all of us.

---

5 Matthew 27:57–60; Luke 23:50–53.
6 Matthew 21:5.
7 Lamentations 3:22–23, New King James Version.

Go out and do good every day. Go out and give someone something they need. Go out and share the abundance He has given you someone else. As God's grace flows into you, don't hoard it. Don't just hold on to it. Let His grace flow through you and out into the world around you. That's how you create a Kingdom Culture here on Earth. That's how you let His will be done, and His kingdom come.

When you shine His light out into the world around you, it shines on the Path of Miracles and reveals the rewards He has waiting for you.

Chapter 52

KINGDOM ECONOMY

There are two types of economic systems. There's an earthly, terrestrial economic system that is managed by supply and demand. And there is a Kingdom Economy that is defined by reaping and sowing.

We all know the first. We live by it every day. You see it at the gas pump all the time. Oil prices go up because more people want it and there is only so much. Everybody pays to reach into the same bucket. Everybody wants some. If the bucket's owner lowers the price, more people can afford some. And vice versa.

So when a lot of people want some, and the owner only has so much to sell, he raises the price to make the most he can. Earthly economics—the monetary, fiduciary, pecuniary, fiscal world—encourages people to charge what the market will bear. The owner will charge as much as people are willing to pay.

Kingdom Economy, and our life, is about reaping and sowing. Whatever you sow you shall reap.[1] Which means the more you put into the bucket, the more you take out. The more you get showered with. The more you put in, the bigger your reward.

In the Kingdom Economy, you pay with your actions, you pay with your deeds, you pay with your thoughts.

You might give actual cash. You might use the currency of the terrestrial, earthly economy to make your contribution. But the difference is, in the Kingdom Economy, you're not putting in cash to buy something in return. You're giving it so that others may use it to go out and do more good things. Even if you give it to someone so they can feed themselves or their family, the

---

1   Galatians 6:7.

end is not the food on the table; the end is the energy that family draws from that food, and how they use that energy to go on and do other things that are good for all humankind. Who knows what those people at that table will be able to accomplish, now that they have sustenance and are able to go forward for at least another day? Or what the world would have lost if they hadn't?

Best of all, in the Kingdom Economy, the less you have when you give, the more you are rewarded. The more it costs you to give to another, the more you will be given. It's proportional, again. In the same way that you can measure the size of your reward by the magnitude of the hell you went through, you can also measure the size of what you reap by what it takes for you to sow it.

> *The Kingdom Economy is defined by reaping and sowing.*

It's not about the total size of what you give. It's about how much it was to you. If a billionaire gives $1 million to charity, that's great. That's a lot. A tremendous amount of good can be done with that, and God will reward that rich man accordingly. But if you give your last penny to help another, or you take your only day off from work to help fix the busted plumbing in an old woman's house, God knows you gave all you had.

The rich man gave a lot, but you gave everything. The rich man will get a lot in return; and you will get everything.

Jesus said so himself, in the Gospel story of the Widow's Mite. A mite was an old coin worth about a half cent. As Jesus stood watching people making offerings at the treasury one day, he saw many giving a lot. Then, an old woman came and gave two mites and Jesus called his disciples around and said, "Truly I say to you, this poor widow put in more than all the contributors to the treasury; for they all put in out of their surplus, but she, out of her poverty, put in all she owned, all she had to live on."[2]

That's why the greatest secret is to give when you have nothing. Because that's your empty tomb giving. It sounds oxymoronic. It sounds absurd. How can you give when you have nothing?

You can. Because you can give hope. And you can give help. And en-

---

2   Mark 12:41–44, King James Version.

couragement, and caring, and companionship. You can pick up a hammer, or pick up a paintbrush, or pick up some trash in the yard. You can help a fatherless child learn to ride a bike—and that's got to be worth at least as much as simply handing out a few dollars so someone else can buy him one.

You can give of yourself, even when you have absolutely nothing else to give. And when you do, when you give of yourself when you have nothing, then God will fill your life—exceedingly, abundantly, above all.

Vertical and Horizontal Living

What we really need to do in our world today, in this miring, confused, and anxious world, in the midst of moral relativism, of wars and tragedies and angst and trepidation, in the midst of all these global anxieties, what we need to do is focus on building a Kingdom Culture through our DNA.

By Kingdom Culture I mean the culture of God's kingdom—of His kingdom come, and His will done, here, on Earth. *Now.*

All we are seeing here on Earth is the physical manifestation of God's desire for His people, for His kingdom. I said that before, in the very beginning of this book. The kingdom of God is not meat or drink, but righteousness, peace, and joy in the Holy Spirit.

What does the Bible tell us?

Thy kingdom come, Thy will be done, on Earth as it is in heaven.

The Lord's Prayer is my personal daily prayer. But not necessarily verbatim every day. It's the Lord's Prayer in sections. I break it down into parts, into thoughts, and I really reflect on what they each mean to me and what I want to say to God about them.

I might begin with "Our Father," and spend an incredible time acknowledging who He is. "Who art in Heaven, hallowed be thy name . . ." It's all about Him. It's praise and it's worship.

"Thy kingdom come . . ." That's where I speak about His kingdom and His will, and I activate that. Worship leads to the kingdom. And by worshipping God I am connecting His kingdom and this world. Of course I am—what does it say?—"Thy kingdom come, Thy will be done, *on Earth as it is in heaven.*"[1]

The kingdom of God has specific principles, Kingdom Principles, that

---

1 Matthew 6:10.

connect heaven to Earth, and us to God. They help us have heaven on Earth. They show us how we should address issues of injustice and poverty, and war and hurt in so many things on this Earth.

I want to see God's principles activated on Earth.

We understand the fall of man. We understand the notion of sin. We understand the idea of mankind's failure and fall. We understand all that, philosophically and theologically.

However, how do we actually get heaven on Earth?

Through vertical and horizontal living.

> **We have both a vertical and horizontal existence.**

I don't find anything to be coincidental in respect to the journey of Christ on this Earth. So, to me, it's not a coincidence that he died on the cross, and that the cross today represents the faith that he founded and all of its followers.

But the cross goes way beyond being just a religious emblem for one of the three major faiths in the world. The cross symbolizes the connectivity between heaven and Earth.

That's the greatest message of the cross: redemption, salvation, and heaven touching Earth. But it also speaks to us in respect to how we should live.

The cross reveals the fact that we actually live a dual life. I don't mean dual in the sense of hypocritical or some sort of fallacy, but rather that we live both vertically and horizontally—that Christ on the cross, life on the cross, shows us how we are supposed to live our lives.

The cross shows us that we have both a vertical and a horizontal existence. We basically live two lives, and the balancing of that life is the secret of success. And the strongest point of our journey here on Earth lies in that nexus, that convergence—at the perfect place where vertical connects with horizontal.

Vertical living means my Godly living—my integrity, my righteousness. It means heaven and my life communicating, and my character reflecting divine principles. It means understanding and upholding the notion of: "Thy kingdom come. Thy will be done *on Earth.*"

Vertical living means to stand upright in all that we do.

Vertical living is love, joy, peace, patience, meekness, goodness, gentleness, temperance, mercy, and faith. Vertical living means concomitant communication with God. It's being crucified daily. It's renewing your mind. It's becoming more like Jesus. It's Galatians 2:20:

"I have been crucified with Christ; and it is no longer I who live, but Christ lives in me; and the life which I now live in the flesh I live by faith in the Son of God, who loved me and gave himself up for me."

Vertical living is my ability to touch heaven. And the reality is that I *can* touch heaven. The fact of the matter is that we have the power of touching heaven. And if there is a free flow in love and in compassion under the canopy of grace, heaven will be touching us continuously.

So it's not only, do I touch heaven? But, *does heaven touch me?* It's more like Jacob's Ladder.[2] There are angels going up and down. There is a continual flow of heaven showering Earth, and Earth sending back to heaven.

Vertical living means exactly that, literally, *vertical* living—standing up living. It means living that is literally not "prone" to the things of the world or the circumstances around us. It is living upright. It is living vertically. It is living, standing up.

That upright piece of the cross is telling us, "Stand up! Face your enemies! Don't give in! Do the right thing! Be not afraid!"[3]

Vertical living means you're not down. You haven't succumbed to the notions, the ideas, the failures. You haven't given in to the defeats. You haven't been overcome by your insecurities, or your circumstances—you're standing up.

Even when Christ was crucified, he was standing up. He was upright. This is not a man on his knees; this is a man standing upright. Even at the moment of death, even in our most difficult circumstance, we can still stand upright.

Standing upright also is synonymous with dignity and virtue. Therefore,

---

2 Genesis 28:11–19.
3 Luke 12:3–5.

vertical living means to stand upright in all that we do, in all of our negotiations, in all of our business dealings, in our family.

We need to ask ourselves every day, are we living vertically? Are we living in a way that touches heaven? And, even more important, are we not just touching it, but are we living in a way that connects heaven with Earth?

That's the difference. It's not just touching heaven—it's connecting heaven with Earth. I don't just want to get on a plane and touch the clouds, I want to build a bridge that continuously exists, that I can cross and connect to, always.

That's vertical living.

> *The perfect life is the life at the nexus of vertical and horizontal living.*

Horizontal living is how I live with those around me. Horizontal living means community. Horizontal living means fellowship. It means fraternity.

Horizontal living means how I treat others. Vertical living is how I treat God and how I treat myself. Horizontal living is how I treat others. How I relate to others. It is my relationship with those around me.

Vertical living talks about redemption and salvation; horizontal living talks about my transformation. To limit our lives only to salvation is only 50 percent of the fight. Redemption and salvation by themselves are wonderful, but we need to add on the horizontal part of transformation—of societal transformation, communal transformation, familial transformation.

If I am living vertically, then I need to evaluate how I am living horizontally. How am I relating to my community? My family? My workplace? My church? My environment? My city? My world? How am I engaged in today's world?

How do I measure this in a practical perspective? Let's go from the theoretical and theological to the practical.

Every single day I evaluate my life vertically and horizontally. How's my relationship with God? How's my relationship with heaven? How's my relationship with eternity? How's my relationship with the divine?

And then I evaluate myself horizontally, where I make sure that horizontally there is good delivery of my vertical living. I look at my thought process. I look at my daily activities.

The strongest point is not where we become so heavenly minded that we do no worse than good, as it has been stated so many times before, but where there is a great balance—at that precise point where the horizontal and the vertical are joined. That connection, that convergence, is the perfect balance. It is perfectly ordered. That's where we can hang everything else. We can hang our dreams and our hopes and our aspirations and our vision on the nexus of vertical and horizontal living.

Life supreme, life par excellence, life purely veritas, life purely truth—the perfect life—is the life at the nexus of vertical and horizontal living.

From the cross comes redemption. And when we have placed our lives perfectly at that spot where the vertical and horizontal are joined, what comes out of us will redeem others. Then what comes out of us will redeem relationships and moments and circumstances. But only if we are perfectly placed on that spot where the horizontal meets the vertical.

> *Vertical living is how I treat God and how I treat myself.*
> *Horizontal living is how I treat others.*

The vertical and the horizontal connect kingdom and society, redemption and relationship, conviction and compassion, *agape* and *philos*, ethos and pathos, pneuma and man, heaven and Earth. The strongest point is the nexus or convergence of both.

Kingdom is vertical, society is horizontal. Conviction is vertical, compassion is horizontal. Ethos is vertical, pathos is horizontal. Righteousness is vertical, justice is horizontal.

And in the religious world, historically what we have done—erroneously— is focused on either/or. We've focused exclusively on: How do I get to heaven? How do I secure eternal life? And we cared only minimally about transforming our surroundings. It's almost an afterthought, a happy accident. We care at a minimal level, and we do not incorporate or invest our time or our resources—intellectual, spiritual, financial, otherwise—in transformation. In the horizontal.

Then there are those who take the other extreme, where everything is horizontal. It's all about Earth. It's all about this life. It's all about community. And nothing about eternity.

Vertical is eternity; horizontal is community. And the moment we are able to channel eternity into the community we are on the Path of Miracles. That's where we activate our path, our passion, our promise, and our purpose—where vertical and horizontal meet.

They meet in this perfect place where we can hang even the heaviest thing on that cross and out of it will come redemption. The pneuma, the spirit, is vertical and the flesh is horizontal, but when they come together in the perfect balance they connect our fleshly deeds with our heavenly purpose, and God's grace and goodness flow through us. Where they meet, our emotions are driven not by our circumstances around us but by the spiritual realities above us and within us. We don't subjugate our emotions, but rather we channel them appropriately, and we invest and divest accordingly.

Prayer is part of that. Prayer and praise are absolutes. In Jacob's Ladder it would be step number one. It's the first thing you must do. It's communication. It's talking to God.

I pray up. I pray vertically. I pray to activate the kingdom. I pray to give thanks. But then I also pray horizontally. I pray for those around me. I pray for their betterment. I pray for their health. I pray that they may be showered with the blessings that I know exist for them.

I also praise up: I acknowledge God. I honor, and I pay tribute. But I also praise—and I say praise not in a way of idolizing or acknowledging of God—but I celebrate the victories of those around me. And every single day I make sure that I acknowledge someone else's victory around me, someone else's success. I look to praise someone.

The power of praising God and praising others around me links me vertically and horizontally to heaven *and* Earth. It's a fundamental communication with God, and a fundamental connection with the people around me.

If we can reconcile both vertical and horizontal living and understand that every single day I live two lives—vertical and horizontal lives—it will transform the way I think, the way I live and the way I treat others.

It will activate the Path of Miracles.

PRINCIPLE SEVEN

YOU ARE ASSURED A FILLED UPPER ROOM

Chapter 54

WHERE THE BREAD IS BROKEN, THE FIRE WILL FALL

The upper room is an interesting place. The upper room is a place for the followers of Jesus, for his disciples. The upper room is the meeting place. It's also the hideout. It was a place of coming together. It's the place where they had the Last Supper,[1] the place where Jesus showed himself to them all after his resurrection,[2] and the place where the Holy Spirit filled them.[3]

It's the place where you have salvation, redemption, and grace personified. Where you have mercy grieving, and resonating, and glowing. Where you have life surrounded by betrayal. Surrounded by denial. Surrounded by faithfulness. Surrounded by stewardship. Surrounded by doubt. Because life is always surrounded by these things.

Let's put this in the Life Surrounded context. Let's not forget that we're no longer looking at these disciples as the followers of Christ, we're looking at them as personality types and embodiments. For example, we no longer see Peter, John, Mark, and Luke, we're seeing the denial and faithfulness, anxiousness and fear—that's what we're seeing from this moment on.

We see that Jesus, prior to his death, met with his disciples in the upper room, and he broke bread with them.

> *The place where you are most attacked is the place where your greatest reward will be.*

---

1 Mark 14:12–14.
2 John 20:19.
3 Acts 2:1–4.

Of course, Jesus means life in the Life Surrounded metaphor. He personifies life. So when we look at Leonardo da Vinci's painting of the Last Supper, what we're actually looking at is life surrounded by the good, the bad, and the ugly.

First of all, notice how life is always in the middle. Life is always in the middle because these things surround life, but life still shines. Life glows with the righteousness, peace, and joy of the Holy Spirit, and life continues to eat and continues to drink, even as he shares his body, his blood, and his spirit with those around him.

So the upper room where we have the Last Supper is the room where we receive that Holy Spirit. The upper room is where we receive everything that God has for us.

Second, notice that the upper room is a place where bread is broken.

Now let me explain that. The biblical narrative of the upper room says the following: They blessed the bread, and they broke the bread.[4] In that order, by the way. That's very important. Because the blessing precedes the brokenness.

At times, our blessed experiences speak to the fact that God wants to do something with our lives where He wants to share our experiences with others. Our breaking seasons and our moments of brokenness speak not to a trial, not just to moments of testing or proving; they really speak to God saying, "I want to share your experience, I want to share My work in you and who I am in you, with you and through you with others. I'm going to bless you to break you."

But this doesn't mean breaking in a way where we collapse into some sort of fetal position and say, "Oh, woe is me!" Brokenness in the hands of God does not necessarily equate with brokenness in the hands of man. Not at all.

God breaking us is not God tearing us apart, but God taking who we are bit by bit, piece by piece, and saying, "I'm going to share a piece of you with someone else, because there's so much life and beauty and power in you. Let me break you."

We all need to go through a breaking experience. It's either going to be God, or it's going to be our circumstances and the things of the world. And

---

4　Matthew 26:26.

I'd rather be broken by God than by the circumstances that surround me, because they don't know how to put me back together. But my Master and my Creator, the Owner of the blueprint, the Engineer, the Architect, knows very well how to put me back together.

> *Where the bread is broken, the fire will fall.*

Luke 22 describes how the disciples gathered around Christ during the Last Supper, and it declares that they would find an upper room where all things would be furnished.

What is God telling us with that? That everything is now ready! We are stepping into a season where all we need is already waiting for us; all we need to do is arrive. You will no longer wait for blessings; blessings will be waiting for you. Every empty place will be filled, every empty wallet, dream, promise, will be filled.

Now, in the literal chronology of the biblical story, the upper room comes ahead of the empty tomb *and* after.

The first time we see the disciples in the upper room, it wasn't filled. Notice the chronological order: First it's blessed, then it's broken, and then it's filled. God will bless us, to break us, to fill us. That's the awesomeness of God.

Do you know what blessing really means? It means that God is going to strengthen us. He is going to give us the anesthesia. He is going to prepare us for surgery. He is going to make sure that we're going to survive this. He'll bless us, and then he'll break us. And then he'll put us together and fill us. But not just fill us. He'll fill us exceedingly, abundantly, and above all.

Then, the Bible says, after He filled them, He set upon them "tongues as of fire."[5] It's saying that tongues of fire descended upon them. But it didn't burn them. No. Because the fire falling is the spirit of God. The fire falling is heaven falling on your Earth. This speaks to the fact that wherever hell descends upon you, if you follow the principles we've outlined here, then heaven will descend upon you. If you see hell, then it's time to see heaven. In the same place.

---

5   Acts 2:3.

Where the bread is broken, the fire will fall. The same place where we experience our breaking moment—not necessarily the physical place, but the same location intrinsically inside of me, the same area of life where I experienced my breaking point—is the same area of life where I will experience my greatest victory.

Now that needs to be underlined, because it speaks to a biblical and a spiritual and a cosmic sense. It's not another area. This area where I experienced my hurt is the same area where I will also experience my joy. We can close experiences, but there are areas of our lives, in our schemata, there are compartments in our lives that we cannot close until God has the final word in that area. Be that a miserable marriage, a terrible relationship, whatever it may be.

Your relationship mantra and the relationship department in your life cannot come to an end until it becomes a viable, joyful, successful relationship. We cannot close areas of our lives until God has filled them.

This whole idea that "I will never trust again!" Well, I've got news for you: Until you learn to trust again and embrace a viable trust that does not betray you, that does not discourage you or abandon you, you're never going to succeed in living exceedingly, abundantly, above all. You're never going to experience your full third day transformation.

Where the bread is broken, the fire will fall. This area that you are attacked in the most is the same area where you will be blessed in the most. So if the greatest area of attack is in your finances, it speaks prophetically to the fact that your finances have been strategically targeted by God to be blessed.

I know it for a fact. It happened to me.

Back in the late nineties, I had the opportunity to found two churches—one in Bethlehem, Pennsylvania, and the other in New York City. Things went along fine until 2000, when I was invited to be a featured speaker at the world gathering of the Assemblies of God, the world's largest Pentecostal denomination.

Talk about a blessing! That took our ministry and created a global platform for us.

Then came the breaking. All hell broke loose in the church we had planted in New York.

I wanted to appoint my sister as a senior pastor, and I would be the overseer. That would allow me to travel as a speaker and still have a headquarters. I did it all within the right process, but there were those who surrounded me in leadership who felt they deserved the senior pastorship. Therefore, things just exploded. My reputation was questioned. My integrity was questioned. There was innuendo. Rumors. Gossip.

Eventually people retracted and they apologized. But it became a very difficult moment of angst, pain, anxiety, and confusion. It was difficult for me, and for my family, but it was the greatest learning experience of my life. I found out I can't preach about the resurrection without preaching about the crucifixion. I found out that I needed to experience my own crucifixion.

And it was the greatest wake-up call from God I could get. Because it was the fear of God instilled in me, on steroids. I found out that I had made ministry and church more important than my three kids and my wife. I had made the church my idol. And that's where God said no. That's where God said, "This is really the right moment to really bring truth to you."

I resigned from that church in New York City. And it was the greatest experience that you must experience the empty tomb before the filled upper room. There is a season where you will run and find nothing right before God runs and gives you everything. But you must be willing to run and find nothing and still keep running. And I learned that for sure.

I had been blessed. I had been broken. And then, God filled me. Right there in the same place, the fire fell.

The chairman of the National Hispanic Christian Leadership Council knew what had happened to me, and he saw it as an opportunity. He saw that it was time to provide national leadership to Hispanic born-again Christians in America, and he said, "We believe that you're it."

In 2001, we moved to California, back on our Path of Miracles.

> *Where you feel the emptiness is where you'll find the upper room.*

That's the way it happens. In our lives, the same place where we experience our breaking moment is the same place where we will have our infilling moment.

Just think about it for a moment. The place where you are most attacked is the place where your greatest reward will be.

If the number-one area in your life that you're weak in is your marriage, then, as incredible as it seems, that's the number-one area God wants to bless you in.

I know what you're thinking: "Sam, wait a second! You're trying to tell me that *because* I've been through my third marriage, and I'm going through hell again, that that's where my greatest reward will be? You're trying to tell me that the number-one area that God wants to bless in my life is my marriage and my relationships? That's pretty amazing."

It is. But it's the truth. Not in spite of the trouble you're having—because of it.

It's a blatant wake-up call. It's not like God is going to straighten you out financially but, unfortunately, leave you with terrible relationships in your life. It's not like it has been prewired for you to have a terrible marriage and that's all there is to it. Nothing you can do. Sorry, that's just the way it is. Everything in your life is wonderful, except for this vitally important central piece of your life.

No. That's not the way it is. The area that you've been attacked in the most is the same area you'll be blessed in the most. Where you feel the emptiness is where you'll find the upper room.

Chapter 55

EMBRACING GOD'S "SUDDENLIES"

Let's look at the upper room story a bit. In the upper room, the biblical narrative states that there are some definitive principles.

The first thing is, there is a "suddenly." The narrative says, "Suddenly, there came a sound like a mighty rushing wind."[1] Verbatim. It became so "suddenly."

God's suddenlies need to be embraced. There are surprises in life that come our way. That turn of events. That unexpected, surprising, spur-of-the-moment incident. Those extraneous and extemporaneous occurrences in our lives need to be embraced. Or at least managed.

Why? Why did it suddenly happen? We weren't expecting that. Why the shift in jobs? Why the sudden unemployment? Why did this person reemerge in my life? These questions need to be analyzed via the prism of the upper room experience, because suddenlies come first. There are things that happen in our lives immediately, out of the blue, out of nothing. And these out-of-nowhere and out-of-nothing experiences speak to God's suddenlies.

> *God is as desperate to be with us and in fellowship with us and to see us fulfill destiny as we are to fulfill destiny.*

Suddenlies are God's surprises for His children. When we least expect it, God will show up. He will show up with manna in the desert, not just with

---

1 Acts 2:2, English Standard Version.

milk and honey in the Promised Land.[2] He will show up in the midst of the storm on the Sea of Galilee, not just in the pinnacle of the temple.

Suddenly your family will be saved. Suddenly your debts will be paid. Suddenly your healing will take place. Suddenly you find peace that surpasses all understanding.

Embrace God's suddenlies.

Second, the biblical narrative goes on to say, "There came a mighty rushing wind." Rushing means God was in a hurry.

Notice how they ran to the empty tomb. Notice how God reciprocated. They ran to Him and God ran to them. God is as desperate to be with us and in fellowship with us and to see us fulfill destiny as we are to fulfill destiny. There is this mutual affinity, a mutual desperation.

God wants to bless us as much as we want to be blessed by Him. Probably more. God wants to be in our presence as much as we want to be in His presence. He wants to walk with us. Just as He walked in the beginning with Adam, He desires and longs to walk with us today. Just as we talk about having a personal relationship with the Almighty, He desires a personal relationship with us.

Let's extend that. It's not only us believing in Him, but Him believing in us. It's not only us trusting God but coming to a point in our relationship where God says: "I trust you. I trust you with this gift. I trust you with this ability. I trust you with this fruit, with this anointing, with this wisdom. I'm entrusting you. I trust you with this intellectual capacity to revolutionize the world. I trust you to lead politically. I trust *you*."

> *In God's orchestra of divinity each and every one of us is a song.*

There is a suddenly, and there is a rush. And then there is a "sound." The Bible says, "There came a sound like a mighty rushing wind."

That sound is very important. The sound speaks to God's melody. To music; to God's song.

Throughout the Psalms, David talks about the "song of the Lord." We all are part of this great musical presentation. And in God's orchestra of divinity each and every one of us is a song. Some of us are love songs. Some of

---

2 Exodus 16:1–35; Exodus 3:8.

us may be country-western. Some may be rock. Some may be hip-hop. But we each represent a song.

Pay close attention to the biblical narrative. The wind itself never filled the upper room. It was the sound. The audible comes before the visible. You have to say it before you see it. Confession precedes realization. Life's sounds precede life's breakthroughs.

Listen to the sound. Listen carefully. Put your ear to the ground and listen to the sound of grace restore the fallen soul. Listen to the sound of mercy reach out to those in need. Listen to the children playing, the wind swaying the trees, the birds singing, and the couples whispering sweet nothings.

The biblical narrative says there came a sound. Then it says that it filled them and then it filled the house.[3]

It filled two things. It filled them individually, and then it filled the house.

They were in the upper room. Christ was crucified. He rose from the dead. The twelve disciples had become one hundred and twenty, who now gathered in the upper room, praying for the fulfillment of what Christ had promised them—that they should receive the Holy Spirit.

Jesus told them, "I am leaving you, but I'm going to send you the comforter. Wait for it. You need to pray and wait for it."

They chose to pray in the same place where the bread was broken the last time they gathered together around life. Because they knew that wherever life was present life leaves an imprint that is transferable for the next generation and for the next step in our lives.

So they went to the place where the bread was broken and, as Acts 2 says, "the Holy Spirit filled them."[4]

It also filled the room. It not only filled them, but it filled their families, the room, their surroundings.

So what happens when we run and find nothing? He runs and gives us everything. Not just what we want and what we need, but exceedingly, abundantly, above all. The dividend return is double what we invested.

> *When we run and find nothing, He runs and gives us everything.*

---

3   Acts 2:2–4.
4   Acts 2:4.

Remember what I told you in Principle 4, Self-Emptying Every Day:

If you have run your course, put your life in order, closed the open chapters, and found nothing, I want you to know that the very next thing that's about to happen in your life is that God is about to run and give you everything. There is always an empty tomb right before a filled upper room.

You are assured of a filled upper room. Assured! And there may be more than one.

Chapter 56

LIFE'S TOUCHSCREEN

The upper room season empowered the disciples. Immediately after they had their upper room season, their upper room experience, immediately after that they began doing something called "the laying on of hands."[1]

It became a practice within the primitive church. And it continues even today within the Pentecostal Charismatic churches of the world. It's not good enough for one to pray for someone else. If you have a need and you come to a Pentecostal Charismatic church they'll never just call you up and say a prayer for you. They take their hands and they place them on you. In the Catholic church, hands are laid on church members at the sacraments of Penance, Confirmation, and Orders.

I find that to be, even outside of the theological ramifications, so unbelievably beautiful. I find it to be so holy, so pure, that two human beings, that adults can interact physically without any notion of sexuality. Or permissiveness. Or lust. That there is a pure platform for human interaction. It's like the child holding a parent's hand as they cross the street, the fatherly embrace.

In this moment, as we become interconnected globally, and as we in the twenty-first-century world experience isolationism as a result of the digital revolution, as we embrace a virtual community rather than a physical reality, we need to remember and utilize the power of human touch. We need to remember the power of Life's Touchscreen.

We need to remember and utilize the power of human touch.

---

1   Acts 8:17.

Life's Touchscreen is the ability to touch someone's heart. It's the ability to touch someone's emotions. It's the ability to touch someone's dream.

We need to embrace Life's Touchscreen.

Ask yourself, "Have I touched someone today?" That's the simplicity of Life's Touchscreen.

Look at the power of a touchscreen in our everyday lives. By me putting my little finger on my iPhone, a number of pictures appear. By just tapping a finger to that phone's touch-sensitive screen I can listen to music. I can see video images. I can access the Web.

Now let's think about this for a second: I can access a global community. I can see images, portraits and pictures of people I love and cherish. All by the touch of my hand.

Similarly, I believe that we have the power to touch areas in our lives and in other people's lives, and activate giftings, abilities, and skills. I believe that we have the ability to activate destiny in people's lives. That's Life's Touchscreen to me. By the touch of my hand, I can activate a song in someone else's life and in my life. I can activate a dream, and I can activate an idea—by human relationships, by connectivity.

Spiritually speaking, I believe that we have the power to touch someone's life and activate positive images, positive music, enriching and engaging and empowering music and images, communities, documents, files and folders— to make a difference in someone's life and, through them, to make a difference in the world. A touch can change someone forever.

I can activate the very contents of our nature—of the God Man in me, of God's Kingdom Culture, of God's DNA. I can activate that, and not only in me, I can activate it in others around me.

That ability was always there by the way. But it required what? A touch. It required interaction. And through that interaction, there is a transaction— a spiritual, emotional, psychological, and physical exchange—that enriches us both.

The transaction requires authorization. It requires validation, authentication of signature. Because I do believe that we have the power of granting authorization on who touches our lives. Any violation of that authorization is confrontation. It's violence. It's war. It's not pretty when there's some sort of theft, aggravated assault, or a stranger who breaks into your home. Anything other than authorized, authenticated, validated access is a crime. Spiritual access or physical access, of my home or of my person. It doesn't matter. If I don't authorize it, it's a violation. It's violence. And it's criminal.

> *Life's Touchscreen is the ability to touch someone's heart. It's the ability to touch someone's emotions. It's the ability to touch someone's dream.*

The inter- and the intradependency of God's creation embedded within His kingdom serves as a warning against the virtual, exclusive community of today, this digital community of today. What we need is not less human interaction. What we need is more human interaction.

I seek it. I anticipate it. I revel in the expectation of the opportunity on a daily basis: Who will God bring me that day? Who will God bring before me? What conversation and what person will enable me to activate and to touch that screen? Who will help me see an image that I have never seen before? Maybe there's another side of beauty that I haven't contemplated yet. Maybe there's another side of peace that I have yet to experience.

That is the power and the reward of Life's Touchscreen, of the simple power of touch—that whatever I do for others will be done unto me. That by activating someone else's destiny my destiny is not only activated, but if my destiny is already activated, there is an exceedingly, abundantly, above all double portion that is poured out over me.

That shouldn't be the primary motivator for me to want to activate someone else. It should not be the reason why I do this. But it is the benefit of what I do. Every time I activate someone else, something is activated within me. Every time I activate, something else saturates my being that is good and is of God—that enriches and empowers and engages and strengthens and protects.

So that's the intrinsic motivation for certain people. I want to activate you because in activating you I activate me even more. But the pure motivation should be just the utter fulfillment of that God gene kicking in, and you experiencing the joy of seeing someone else accomplish his or her dream.

In the touchscreen there is an embedded life principle: Preposterous as it may sound, I want to touch someone's life in order for that life to go further than anywhere I have gone.

I know that sounds absurd, the idea of wanting someone else to have and be and accomplish more than me. But there's a biblical precedent. John the Baptist prepared the way for Jesus. He said, "the One who is coming is mightier than I."[2]

As a matter of fact, John said, in so many words: "The person who follows me, I am not worthy of tying his sandals. I baptize you with water for repentance. But he is going to baptize you in the Holy Spirit and fire."[3]

Basically what he was saying was, "You think I'm good? You haven't seen *anything* yet. Coming behind me is something even greater."

He knew. And he knew that that meant he had succeeded—because what followed was even greater than him.

> *Anytime I activate someone else, it enriches me.*

Here's how I measure success. I don't measure success by short-term metrics. I argue that it is impossible to measure success with short-term metrics. Utterly impossible to say, "I am successful." Utterly impossible for the New York Yankees to say after ten games, "We're ten—and—0 this season. That means we're the World Series champions."

After ten games! They can't. It is impossible to measure success in the short term. Utterly impossible.

The real way of measuring success—be it for a corporation, a ministry, a church, a business, or a life—is not by the metrics you establish for yourself in the short term, but rather whether those who follow you are greater than yourself. That's the great metric of success. That's how you measure it.

Let's look at this crazy thing we call Christianity. It started with one revolutionary man—this great philosopher, rabbi, teacher. One man, who found twelve people to join him to spread the word. Not the cream of the crop, by the way, just twelve Jewish men from the Middle East.

Two thousand years later, here we are. It's still around. It's not only around, but in Africa and Latin America it is flourishing in unprecedented numbers: with over a billion members, Christianity is the largest faith system in the world!

So, what followed that one man?

---

2   Luke 3:16.
3   Luke 3:16.

He even said, "Hey, greater works you will do in my name, for I go to the Father."

Greater works. That's amazing.

How do we know we're successful? When what follows us is greater than ourselves.

My father would always say, I want to make sure that you go further, at every level—academically, financially, your career, with your family—than I've been able to give you. I want you to provide more for yours than I've been able to provide for you. So I'm going to work hard to make sure that you go further than I've gone.

And I am committed to making sure my children go further than I go. I want my son to be a better father. I want my son to be a better husband. I want my son to be a better child of God. I want my son to be a better agent of transformation and change. I want my son to live exceedingly, abundantly, above all, even much more than I've experienced.

I want my daughter to do the same.

> *Our success is measured by the success of those who follow us.*

That's how you measure success. That's Life's Touchscreen: touching people so they can go further; touching people so they can leave a legacy and they can measure success by making sure that those who follow are greater than themselves.

Now if we were to apply that to our families, even to our corporations, what can happen? Can you imagine a CEO who begins to mentor his successor and says, "Listen, son, I'm not going to be here forever. And I'm never going to be remembered as a great CEO until you become better than I."

That's an amazing story. Apply that to any field of your choice. To any calling of your choice. What is the potential? What happens when the multiplicative effect of my touch and your touch and the touch of those who follow us combines?

Our success is measured by the success of those who follow us. If not, what we did was we built our own personal fiefdoms and kingdoms, and it was all about us. It was selfish, prideful, arrogant regurgitation of an old modality, of an archaic way of thinking, where it begins and it ends with us.

We must extend the continuum and we must extend the narrative so that we know that those who follow will carry that narrative in their hard drive, and they will add to it and take it further than we ever could have, and then they will transfer that over onto those who follow them.

You have to make sure that those who inherit it from you go even further. Can we facilitate a platform so that those who follow us can be greater than ourselves? Can we facilitate relationships? Can we create the structures and the systems to assure that those who follow us can go further than ourselves?

That is what leads to the filled upper room. It is the commitment of the one who did it all and accomplished it all, and states: "Now I'm going to have to leave, for you to go further. Now that I've won the prize, I not only give you the trophy, but it's for you to enjoy the reward—with the commitment that you will go further."

Chapter 57

DOUBLE PORTIONS

Jesus appeared to the disciples twice in the upper room.[1] Both times Peter was there. But Christ didn't say anything about Peter having denied him three times. Jesus had told him he was going to be in that same room, but he didn't say anything about it when he saw him there.

The next time he appeared to Peter, though, was at the Sea of Tiberias,[2] standing on the shore at dawn—the same lake where Peter had tried and failed to walk on water. It is not a coincidence that in the same place where Peter failed, Christ appeared to him again, and this time he called him out. In the same identical place.

There it is again: The same place where we fail in our lives is where we have our greatest success. The same place in our lives where we have our failures also has the same potential to give us our greatest miracle.

> *For every single day that you have been down,*
> *you can have one thousand days when you're up.*

Sometimes in life we look for a different venue. We say, "There is no way in the world this event, this moment, this tragedy, this circumstance in my life can produce anything good. So let me compartmentalize it, let me categorize it, let me put a stamp on it, seal it down with latches and keys, throw away the keys, put it in my memory bank. And let's make sure it's never touched again."

---

1   John 20:19; John 20:26.
2   John 21:1.

But in reality, regardless of how difficult it may be, and I know it sounds absurd, but every single place where you may have fallen or there may have been great pain carries the potential of actually giving you your greatest miracle.

So Jesus confronts Peter in the same place where he walked and fell. And now Peter is stripped naked. This fisherman who had denied Christ is naked, stripped, in more ways than one. He was stripped of his place in this viable ministry, where we see so much media attention and the accolades of the crowd. He was stripped of his fame. He was stripped of his popularity. He was stripped of the financial income streams that guaranteed his security and viability financially for him and his family. He was stripped of his repute.

And Jesus asks him three times, in order to equate to the three times Peter denied him, "Do you love me?"[3]

He says, "Peter, I'm going to fix what just happened. Remember how you denied me three times? Watch this: Do you love me?"

"Yes, I do."

There goes the first one.

"Do you love me?"

"Yes, I do, Lord."

There goes the second one.

"Do you love me?"

"Of course. I said I do, Master."

There goes the third one.

And Jesus says, basically, "Peter, we're even. Thank you very much."

And there is this great moment, this great epiphany, this great moment of restoration, this great, I got it! moment.

Now Peter stands up. He's restored, and he's activated.

Now notice how Peter, just a few days before, was one of the runners who experienced the empty tomb experience. But it takes this confrontation—here it goes again: confrontation, revelation, activation—it takes this confrontation and revelation to bring his activation. Because sometimes we have to hit that wall hard in order to wake up. Sometimes we have to hit that hard place, have that moment of intervention, in order to wake up.

---

3   John 21:15–17.

> *Sometimes we have to hit that hard wall in order to wake up.*

Peter gets restored. So he preaches his first sermon, and three thousand people are changed.[4] Now let's go back: How many times did Peter deny Jesus? Three. And how many people responded to his first sermon and were transformed? Three *thousand*—one thousand for every time he denied Jesus.

It's not a coincidence. It's a lesson: For every single day you have been down, you can have one thousand days when you're up. For every single day you've been broken, you'll have one thousand days when you're whole. For every single day you lamented and mourned, you'll have one thousand days of dancing. For every day you had a door closed before you? One thousand days of having doors open.

You can continue that with a litany of things. For every day of no, one thousand days of yeses.

In fact, one of the editors of this book discovered the truth about God's double portions—literally.

Less than a year after he was married, doctors diagnosed Kevin Carrizo di Camillo with testicular cancer. They caught it early, but he faced a dilemma: He and his wife wanted children. But the treatment required surgery, followed by a month of radiation therapy that could leave him sterile. As practicing Catholics, neither Kevin nor his wife could agree to forgo a church ban on freezing some of his sperm as a backup.

He beat the cancer. But visits to various specialists confirmed their fears. Kevin was totally sterile.

To make things worse, the cancer treatment wrecked them financially. Even with health insurance, the costs were astronomical. The weeks dragged into months and then years, and their prayers remained unanswered. Science seemed to have the last word: they could not have a child. With medical bills draining their finances, Kevin and his wife didn't have any extra money to adopt through an adoption agency.

But they never gave up. They started taking state-sponsored foster parent and foster-to-adopt classes. And they continued to pray: "God, if it is your will, please give us a child."

---

4   Acts 2:14–41.

He didn't. For four years, they prayed—they ran and found nothing.

Then, their prayers were answered, in double portions.

"He gave us *twin* newborn infants—a boy and a girl, six days old, both perfectly healthy," Kevin says.

God's gifts didn't stop there. Since the children were "wards of the state," the state paid Kevin and his wife over a thousand dollars a month to help raise them. The state also covered medical insurance, food and milk, and things like car seats, strollers, and high chairs.

Plus, even after Kevin and his wife formally adopted the children, the state agreed to pay for day care for the twins for five years—the equivalent of about $72,000.

That's exceedingly, abundantly, above all.

Chapter 58

SPIRITUAL UPGRADES

Prior to the upper room the disciples said, "If I see you, Christ, I will follow you." And they followed him everywhere. (Except, of course, to the cross.)

After the upper room experience, there's a shift. There's a spiritual upgrade. After the empty tomb, and the gathering in the upper room, and the mighty rushing wind, they say, "You're in me. I no longer need to see it to believe it. You're in me."

Spiritual upgrades speak to the notion presented in the book of Acts of "signs and wonders."

Before, I followed Jesus. Now that Jesus is in me, I'm being followed. Before, I followed Christ, prior to the empty tomb and upper room. Now that he lives in me there are things following me. And the things that follow me are goodness and mercy, signs and wonders.

> *When you activate the Kingdom Principles, goodness and mercy,*
> *signs and wonders will follow you.*

Wherever I go I am being followed. The Bible says, "goodness and mercy shall follow me all the days of my life."[1] So I am being followed by goodness and mercy.

But what we need to do is enter into that dimension where we truly activate that principle. There are people who are continuously followed by failure, by defeat, by depression and discouragement and excitement and fear

---

1   Psalm 23:5–6, King James Version.

and confusion and disappointment. But when you activate the Kingdom Principles, when you activate the upper room reality, when you activate these truths, goodness and mercy, signs and wonders will follow you.

Goodness is self-explanatory. Mercy is self-explanatory. Signs and wonders are not.

Signs, by their very definition, point. They give direction. Once we activate the Kingdom Principles and have our empty tomb, upper room experience, we achieve our spiritual upgrades, and we become beacons for others. We will know the way. We will know the direction God intended for us to go. We will know the road He planned for us to follow. We will know the Path of Miracles.

We will know the true direction for His kingdom to come and His will to be done here on Earth, and others will see that we know and they will follow us. After we achieve our spiritual upgrades, we all will have followers somewhere in our lives.

Not that we are quasi-messiahs or we're little messiahs. No, but we do have followers. Somewhere in our lives, we will exert some sort of leadership. Regardless of who we are.

The usual modality would be as a father or a mother, as a parent. Our children follow us. They follow us; we provide leadership. But we want to be sure that we're leading those who follow us to the right place. With the right motivation. Under the right canopy. With the right values. At the right time.

And that's where signs come in. Signs point the direction for us, so that we can point the direction for others. Signs show us the path, so we can lead the way. Signs show us, so that we don't go astray.

> *Once we achieve our spiritual upgrades, we become beacons for others.*

Then there are wonders. The Bible says, "signs *and* wonders."[2]

The wonders are these extemporaneous manifestations of God's grace. They are those events, incidents and moments when we have to go, "I wonder how that happened?" And, we wonder, "Why?"

Wonders are those things that make us shake our heads and realize that

---

2   Acts 5:12, King James Version.

there is a power greater than ourselves, and to be thankful that He is watching over us. It's the instances when we think, "I can't believe it. I can't believe God got me out of this. I can't believe He would do this for me."

It's those circumstances—big and small—where there is no way we can give anyone else the credit but Him.

But there are people who still doubt. They see those signs. They see those wonders. And they call it coincidence. Or they are blind to it.

After your spiritual upgrade, their blinders will come off. The veils will be lifted. The smoke will clear. It may not happen all at once but, soon enough, they'll begin to see the undeniable change in you, the transformation that makes you so totally different now, and how you are constantly being showered by God's gifts.

Remember that old saying, "Smile. It makes them wonder what you're up to."

It's true. When they see your smile, they'll wonder. When they see your inner peace, your calm and your confidence, they'll be curious. And when they see how easy life has become for you, how effortlessly you succeed, they'll want to follow.

Daily, there will be opportunities to provide direction for others through signs. Daily, there will be wonders.

God is going to do at least one wonderful thing every day. What we need to do is be open, be sensitive enough to identify that wondrous demonstration of God's grace and mercy in our lives. It occurs daily.

I see it in my little daughter's eyes when I see her come home from school and demonstrate joy. I see it in my seventeen-year-old high school graduate's face as she struggles between the fact that she is entering definitive adulthood, yet at the same time she still looks at me with eyes that say, "Daddy, don't let go of your baby girl."

I see it in the Wow! moment. I see it in my wife's smile when we're playing volleyball in the backyard together.

I see God's wonder every day.

I see it every time we reach out to those in need. I see it every time we see a smile on a child who's impoverished and we provide some sort of resource—even if it's only for a day or a week or a month. I see it in the little things and I see it in the big things. I see it in the individual accomplishments and doings and acts. And I see it corporately.

That's where I see it. Whenever we restore a smile and bring a couple one step closer together, and their troubled marriage one step further away from divorce. When we give hope to a young man who was involved in gangs and tell him, "You may have grown up without a father, but one day you'll be a wonderful father—if you follow the Father and adhere to the following principles. Your true heritage does not come from the father who abandoned you, but rather, the Father who has created an incredible future for you. You have the ability within you to change your destiny."

I see God's wonder in that. I see it in the businessman who successfully contracts a brand-new deal and takes his corporation to the next level. And I see it in the person who dreamt so many times, who tried again and again, and found so many empty tombs but finally, finally, finally reached the upper room and says, "I'm glad I never gave up."

These are the wonders. These are the wonders that we can see every day. They are the result of the spiritual upgrades. Because prior to the upper room and prior to the empty tomb we were the ones following. And now these wonders follow us.

> *God's mercies are new every morning.*

One of the important factors for getting spiritual upgrades is location, location, location. You must be able to restore the place that was broken— meaning that the place where the bread was broken is the same place where the fire will fall.

In other words, the same place where you have the last supper, the same place where life is surrounded, is the same place where you will receive the spiritual upgrades. When I go there I will receive the spiritual upgrades. Then I will get those additional blessings.

It's all about putting ourselves in the right place spiritually, and repositioning our lives. Before, we were still being followed by our past and our failures and our anxieties and our insecurities and our shortcomings. Now I look back and what do I see? Signs, wonders, goodness, and mercy.

I always make sure mercy stays closest to me. Because if I ever fall or have some sort of a misstep, signs and wonders will do me no good. And goodness may be good, but I need mercy to pick me up.

That's why. Out of all of them, the only one that the Bible says is new every single morning is mercy.[3] Because His mercies are new every morning, every morning God is ready to pick us up if we fall. To help us out in our time of need. To push us in the times when we fall a little behind. His mercies are new every morning.

Every morning, embrace mercy. Tell mercy, "Follow me."

---

3   Lamentations 3:22–23, English Standard Version.

Chapter 59

THE MARATHON OF MIRACLES

There is a marathon of miracles for those willing to run. There is a marathon of opportunities, open doors and unbridled blessings for those willing to run.

God put opportunities and miracles out there for us—in the uncommon place, and in our path. But only those who are willing to run while it's still dark, even in their darkest hour, can find them.

Life and God together laid out a plethora of miracles that are there only for those who have the audacity to run while it is still dark. Peter, Mary Magdalene, and John ran in the darkest hour, and they encountered a powerful truth: life everlasting. Eternity. They discovered resurrection. They discovered coming back. They discovered life again. New life. And they discovered it when they were willing to run when others were not.

> *I am not waiting for a miracle; there is already a*
> *miracle waiting for me.*

I believe the Lord has placed things in our journey, and if we run when it is still dark these things become exposed.

We need to find the miracle in the unexpected place. It's not going to be in the commonplace. The miracle will be found in the uncommon place.

But it is there. It is waiting for me to find it. And I need to know that this day will offer me opportunities to find a miracle.

God is not saying to me, I'm going to offer you an opportunity and a miracle per week. He's not saying, "I'm going to offer you an opportunity and a miracle per month." No. Every single day there's a miracle waiting for me.

Underline that: <u>I am not waiting for a miracle; there is already a miracle waiting for me.</u>

It's not like I have to ask. I don't have to say, "God, please. I need a miracle." The miracle is already there. It's a matter of discovering the miracle. Not receiving it, but discovering it. The miracles are out there. It's my job to find them.

Every single day there's a miracle out there for you and me to discover. Through a relationship, through a conversation, through an encounter. They may seem serendipitous, but it's actually preordained. There are miracles out there waiting for us. A miracle of life. A miracle of love. A miracle of relationships. That house. That new job opportunity.

They are there waiting for me already, and I will discover a new one every day, once the Kingdom Principles are completely activated. It's like turning on a flashlight in a dark tunnel. I can see where to go, and I can see the rewards that were hidden. It's all clear.

And I did it for myself. I turned on the light. I activated the principles in my life. I activated my Spiritual DNA. I created the right atmosphere for my God genes to flourish. I made sure all the spots were filled in my Life Surrounded. I live vertically and horizontally.

All of that leads me on the journey that God wanted me to take, following the path He intended for me, to fulfill my purpose. As I follow that path, I will discover the miracles He set out for me before I even took the first step.

That's the key. I'm doing it for myself. I'm finding the miracles. I didn't wait for them to be handed to me. I didn't ask God to give me a miracle. I didn't ask God to do my work for me. I go out and find the miracles for myself, every day. And every day I find more. It's a never-ending marathon of miracles, just waiting for me to discover them.

There is a marathon of miracles out there, and all of God's blessings and all of God's gifts. I was born to have them showered down upon me.

And once I'm on the Path of Miracles, I can't stop. I can't say, "I made it, there's the daybreak. Okay, I quit. That's it. I'm done."

No. No. No. No. No. Because it's exceedingly, abundantly, above all. It's a marathon of miracles, not just one. There is a multitude of daybreaks, not just one.

Let's not forget that every single daybreak introduces new opportunities. Greater opportunities. Greater enrichment. Greater relationships. Greater empowerment. Every day, every single day, every single daybreak, enables you to see more of God. To absorb more of God. More of God's kingdom becomes alive every single daybreak.

> *There is a marathon of miracles out there, and all of God's blessings and all of God's gifts. I was born to have them showered down upon me.*

But every single daybreak that you give up, that's a daybreak when you let your miracles just fade away. Every day that you quit, that you don't give it your all, that you let your flesh overrule your spirit, that you don't activate the Kingdom Principles in your life, is a day when the miracles remain hidden. Because you're not waiting for a miracle, there is a miracle waiting for you—and it's totally up to you to go get it. If you give up, you can't.

I have to follow the right path and follow the Kingdom Principles, if I want to find the miracles. I'm not praying for my miracle anymore. I'm going to pray for God to give me the energy and the strength and the wherewithal to activate His DNA inside of me, so I can go and grab my miracle.

Then I'm going to go out and do it.

I'm not going to pray for God to change my circumstances, I'm going to pray for God to change and equip me so I can change the circumstances. Because the moment I change, that circumstance will forevermore be changed.

It's about me. That circumstance speaks to who I am and what I can be. I am what matters.

I am the one on the Path of Miracles.